Unrolled Stone

Heidegger's *Being and Time*,
Brian Jones, and the Rolling Stones

"I fancy that the faces which look out at us from the past are
the surest indication we have of the meaning of an epoch."
Kenneth Clark, *Civilisation*

By
L.T. Stallings

Abridged Edition

© 2015, L.T. Stallings
Published and Printed by:
BoD – Books on Demand, Norderstedt
Printed in Germany
ISBN 978-3-7392-1699-7

CONTENTS

Frontispiece…i

Dedication…ii

Acknowledgements…iii

My Personal Journey to the East – The Life and Death of a Burning Idea…v

Preface (a portion)…xi

Preface: The Dis-ease of the Times…xiii

Note…xxii

The Précis, How to Read It, or Not Read It: An Excursus…xxiii

Original Cover…xxvi

Précis…1

"Adonais" by P.B. Shelley…40

Scapegoat…42

The Scream…43

In Track of a Shadow…45

Tightrope Ride…97

Is Nothing Sacred?…99

Annex…100

Recommended Reading…126

The Spirit of '76 – A Biographical Sketch…128

An American Dream?…130

Personal / General…131

FRONTISPIECE

To Paul Demeny   Charleville 15 May 1871

"…The Poet makes himself a SEER through a long, tremendous, planned DERANGEMENT of ALL THE SENSES. All the forms of love, of suffering, of madness: he himself seeks and in himself exhausts all poisons, so as to keep only the quintessences. Ineffable torture that takes all his faith, all his superhuman strength, that makes him, among his fellow-men, the great Sick Man, the great Criminal, the great Accursed – and the supreme Sage! – For he reaches the UNKNOWN. Because he has cultivated his soul, rich already, more than anyone else! He reaches the unknown, and if, maddened in his pursuit, he should in the end lose all understanding of his visions, still he has seen them! Let him perish in his fling through things unheard-of and unnameable; other terrible toilers will come; they will start out from the horizons where he succumbed! … "

Arthur Rimbaud (1854-1891)

(see E. Kahler, *The Tower and the Abyss*, pp. 137-138)

DEDICATION

In a spirit of respectful admiration, this book is dedicated to the memory of MARTIN HEIDEGGER, who has so radically illuminated the shimmering horizon of the historical present, and to the ROLLING STONES themselves, who have dared to grope so courageously toward its ever-evasive irresistibility.

"Our destiny exercises its influence over us even when, as yet, we have not learned its nature: it is our future that lays down the law of our today." – Friedrich Nietzsche

ACKNOWLEDGEMENTS

I am humbly indebted to and gratefully salute three illustrious teachers whose Socratic midwifery has been especially crucial in the critical steps of my own thinking development:

Professor Charles Drekmeier of Stanford University

Professor Albert Borgmann of the University of Montana (formerly of the University of Hawaii)

Professor J. L. Mehta of both the University of Hawaii and Harvard University

Sine quibus non

"Came Neptunus
    his mind leaping
        like dolphins…" – Ezra Pound

A FINAL ACKNOWLEDGEMENT

I would like to take this last opportunity to profusely thank Lucas Kent Ogden for his incredible exertions and labors on my behalf in the preparation and publication of this new version of *Unrolled Stone*.

A gentleman, scholar, and dear friend, without his undying help, support, and advice, this book would <u>never</u> have seen the light of day.

He understood perfectly that the Sixties were a spiritual stampede of power, depth, and creativity on all fronts, especially in the field of music. More than a historical event, they represent a permanent possibility of the human spirit, and an expansion of consciousness. They can be reactivated and embodied any where, any time, by any and every body. In short, a cultural and spiritual heritage that can never die.

Thanking you once again for everything you have done for me… My life has been enriched by your presence…

Sine quo non

*P.S. – I would also like to thank Daniel Schottmüller for a last-minute proof-reading of the entire book. He not only went over the text with a fine-tooth comb, but as a stickler for detail he has a truly microscopic eye. Superb job, thank you so much!

"There's no success like failure, and failure's no success at all."
– Bob Dylan

***My Personal Journey to the East –
The Life and Death of a Burning Idea***

To the Reader,

I hereby put into your hands a work that has been the labor of a lifetime. If you derive as much pleasure in reading it as I did in writing it, my gargantuan efforts on your behalf will have been more than rewarded.

Let me explain…

The *theme* of Unrolled Stone as a book is TECHNOLOGY and NIHILISM, the deepening existential crisis, relativity, and collapse of the highest values in our time – an AXIOLOGICAL meditation (moral, aesthetic, religious, and metaphysical – the "polytheism" of values).

The *dramatis personae* are: Martin Heidegger, Brian Jones, and the Rolling Stones.

Unrolled Stone as it now stands, after a hiatus of more than 40 years, I will try to publish once again. The structure is basically a triptych consisting of:

1) A *Précis* (written in 1971 – 50 pages).
2) *In Track of a Shadow* (written in 1972 – 50 pages).
3) An *Annex* (compiled in 2015).

My own interest in the Rolling Stones goes back to early 1964 when they first cut "Not Fade Away," and I have taken great pains to minutely follow their step by step total development with passionate precision ever since (even to the extent of walking across campus in Hawaii to my graduate philosophy seminars in the mid-1960's with a copy of *16*, *Fave*, or *Rave* magazine under my arm if a peripheral article or newsy item had turned up on the Stones in a particular issue).

So it need hardly be said that *Unrolled Stone* is not merely a flash-in-the-pan or fly-by-night affair. My own remarks from a July 29th, 1966, newspaper review of the first Rolling Stones' concert in Honolulu (cited on p. 20 of the *Précis*) should be sufficient enough objective evidence to belie such an assertion. Throughout the five year course of Ph.D. studies in Comparative Philosophy at the East-West Center, U. of Hawaii, where I specialized in Contemporary

European and Indian Philosophy, the germ of *Unrolled Stone* slowly unfolded with a quasi-conscious surety – until near the end of 1971.

I decided then and there to postpone the imminent completion of a doctorate in Germany, because I strongly felt that such a novel book on the Rolling Stones had to be written before all else, had to be done NOW at the most relevant historical moment possible. Why? Because I saw with a blinding clarity that what the *Rolling Stones* were SINGING about (with its Blues foundation) was IDENTICAL with what HEIDEGGER was WRITING about in *Being and Time* (a FUSION of HORIZONS).

I was so convinced by the truth and rightness of my insights, that in September 1971 I flew from Hawaii back to the mainland, and then hitchhiked non-stop across America on the Interstate 80 highway from Sather Gate on the U.C. Berkeley campus to the George Washington Bridge (San Francisco → New York City – a 3000 mile journey to the East in 7 days). Why I did this was simple and clear – I wanted to get in touch and stay in touch with leading New York publishers in person.

Therefore, after some trials and tribulations, I managed to get settled down, and compose a detailed *Précis* (basically a fairly rigorous outline, a philosophically-inspired overview of *Unrolled Stone*), which I nevertheless believed was watered down enough to be sufficiently intelligible to any moderately attuned senior editor. I submitted the said *Précis* to Harper & Row, and five other big-name publishing houses in New York in 1972. Only Harper expressed a really genuine interest in financially supporting such a unique book, and they asked me at the end of the Stones' *Exile on Mainstreet* tour that summer (1972) to write up an actual sample chapter from the book – which I duly submitted that November (1972) entitled *In Track of a Shadow* (essentially an intricate elucidation of the song "Paint It Black" that stresses Brian Jones' crucial role in the song's eery genesis). In this respect *In Track of a Shadow* is a concrete extension of the *Précis* to *Unrolled Stone*.

      The sample chapter, the centerpiece, the jewel in the crown of the triptych that is *Unrolled Stone*, also represents a stylistic experiment in language whose incipient radicality I hope can be appreciated. Indeed I can honestly say that every word has been thought out in terms of its subtlety and potential richness. In other words, I don't think there is a wasted word in the whole chapter. In this age of the obvious decline of language, language itself must be *re*-juvenated, be *re*-imbued with the artistic power to really speak, to literally generate 'reality.' This means that any writer has an awesome professional responsibility that cannot be shirked, for as Nietzsche has said, "every word is a prejudice."

Leaving aside all feigned sense of modesty, I firmly believed that *Unrolled Stone* would be quite simply *the* definitive work on the Rolling Stones. The Rolling Stones would HAPPEN in the book that comes THROUGH me. The TEXT would be the thing that has happened.

But I was faced with a pressing, yet fundamental problem, which was simply this: MONEY (and hence by implication TIME). The big-name publishers with enough money to advance for the completion of *Unrolled Stone* were too narrow mindedly conservative and short sighted to see the patently obvious existential import of this book, while the smaller publishing companies, although far more flexible and open-minded, simply did not have the necessary available funds to adequately back such a venture.

In short, I was left hanging, my burning idea, my dream, died, not even stillborn (à la David Hume's *Treatise On Human Nature*), but *not* born at all. I was forced by circumstance to give up my project at the end of 1973, and resume my graduate studies in philosophy in Germany at the beginning of 1974. The cost in TIME and ENERGY had been immense, over two years (1971, 1972, and 1973).

Concluding Remarks

However, all is not lost. I still have the manuscript in two parts, a *Précis*, and a sample chapter, *In Track of a Shadow* – a total of around 100 pages. Although not a book, but an amputated TORSO, or a book PROJECT, I still believe its basic insights are valid and true as far as they go even today, perhaps even more so than ever today.

So what I have done this year is to compile an Annex. Its purpose is twofold: to flesh out the *Zeitgeist* ("spirit of the times"), the framework, the backdrop, the *Weltanschauung* ("worldview") existing back then, and to show how a book project like *Unrolled Stone* came into being, its GENESIS as it were.

The documentation thus presented, exhibited, is varied. It consists almost entirely of my own writings of the time 1971-1973.

And so dear reader I take leave of you now, hoping that *Unrolled Stone* will resonate, echo within you as it has for me all these years… Fare Thee Well…

    L.T.S.

Tübingen, Germany   June 16, 2015

*Note – For those of you who want more of the same, I urge you to consult the complete version of *Unrolled Stone*. There you will find almost 70 pages of extra text that can be perused at your leisure (poems, articles, and letters).

PREFACE (a portion)

In terms of the current temporal interplay of a receding horizon of over-arching meaning and its shuddering result – namely an underlying, concrete historicity – one dominant question continues to hauntingly animate the interpretive thrust of this book: what are the fateful conditions for the possibility of someone like a ROLLING STONE? Even though it is stated in a provisionally Kantian manner, clearly this is no ordinary question, however much it might seem so to the thoughtless and the un-receptive who typify much of the insensitive "dead weight" of the present. For in its very asking is embedded much of the RADICAL UPROOTEDNESS of our own age, the age of the planetary collision between modern man and global technology in the retrogressive context of a darkening world relentlessly metamorphosing itself into a flattened-out, valueless, pure mathematical present (this exhaustive and exhausting process of "de-spiritualization" obscenely parades itself naïvely under the euphemism of "progress"). It is precisely in its UNROLLING through the life-stretch of a single yet significant human being that this unordinary QUESTION acquires the status of a productive MARK which can only be glimpsed in the form of an incisive PORTRAIT.

If the reader will but dis-cover some jagged fragments of his own life-history in the gathering sweep of this study, then the author feels that the book will have more than accomplished its exploratory task: to wit, an ILLUMINATION of the commonality of individual fates that dovetail inexorably into a generational rubric that can be called a "DESTINY." We shall be 'on the way to wisdom' when we thinkingly accept the loosened shackles of our own fatefully binding destiny, for it is assuredly only the felt resistance of these never-to-be-fully-broken chains that will allow us to dance with the tranquil, yet joyous fervor of a *Zarathustra*, a *Zorba*, or a *Jumpin' Jack Flash*. This is the passionate freedom which does not so much break with and thus shatter tradition altogether, as it does re-appropriate the waiting claim of that same heritage in ever novel, yet authentic ways. It is only in such a manner that we can even begin to step beyond the shrill, paralyzing nihilism of our essentially "belongingless age," the age of the Rolling Stones… "Into each new home we must take the old gods with us" (Wilhelm Dilthey's essay "The Dream" – cf. H. Meyerhoff's *The Philosophy of History In Our Time*).

"What does nihilism mean?
THAT THE HIGHEST VALUES
DEVALUATE THEMSELVES,
The aim is lacking: 'WHY?'
finds no answer." – Friedrich Nietzsche

"I wish I never left home." – Brian Jones

PREFACE: The Dis-ease of the Times

For an increasing many of us today the most thought-provoking thing about this essentially thoughtless age is that we are in danger of suffocating within the iron grip of invisible powers and opaque forces utterly beyond the control, ken, and call of anyone. Indeed, the uncanny 'logic' of contemporary events simply reinforces a pervasive feeling already tinged with deep disquiet, angry outrage, and paralyzing despair: namely, that a full-blown nihilism as the 'normal' condition of man is being blindly forged out of the sagging crucible of our precarious era.

In barely disguised, lonely desperation we linger in the heartland of a technocratic void which rides roughshod over the fragile aspirations of an emerging humanity, and which with equal mindlessness mutilates the vulnerable ecological body of Nature on the grim rack of economic 'necessity.' Our institutions – whether we speak about the family, the school, the church, the university, the labor union, the business corporation, the governmental agency, or the State – have degenerated into little more than reciprocal and overlapping networks of internalized violence; while directionless 'leaders' either urge us to glut ourselves aimlessly at the expense of others, or mouth jellied clichés squeezed from the exhausted residue of an ossified past. Our jobs have become psychic prisons chaining us to the treadmill of a meandering oblivion, and we are in effect bludgeoned in order to march in thudding step to a straightjacket conformity which is 'killing' time while time kills us. Mind-suicide would seem to be the indispensable precondition for the perpetuation of a much emulated, swinish contentedness and its necessary correlate – a dubious sanity.

    If we step back, however momentarily, from the subliminal din of advertising, with its busyness-as-usual 'ethic' doggedly bombarding the innermost recesses of our fleeting, personal lives, at some point we are forced by our own integrity to raise certain fundamental questions concerning the undeniable bankruptcy and shipwreck of our own age: Who are we? Where are we going? What is the point of it all? If we go further and attempt to shake the bars of the elaborate cages that have been so carefully constructed for us by the mysterious machinations of self-deceptive, calculating others, we are told that it is rude and even 'unreasonable' to be so shrill. Moreover, to persist in such behavior and refuse to be co-opted is tantamount to being relegated to the supine position of a random psychiatric couch, or guilty genuflection before the forgiving intolerance of an all-embracing, glassy theological gaze.

At least this much is certain: we have understood better than our elders in the very guts of our daily lives the 'death of God,' and have experienced the numbing tug of the absurd as it draws us into the gaping jaws of a crystalline nothingness. The Bomb and boredom – these are the existential absolutes between which we are challenged to chart the hazardous course of a potentially authentic, common 'destiny' on a choppy sea rife with uncertainty.

Although it would be sheer mystification to expect a beplumed phoenix of hope to emerge magically and unscathed from the scattered ashes of our historical epoch, nevertheless certain striking traces or iridescent striations are becoming more and more clearly distinguishable on the groundless bedrock of the immediate present. For example, viewed from the intimate standpoint of an atrophied and dying dominant culture which is fed by the yawning hiatus between private isolation and public chaos, perhaps the most singularly significant phenomenon of recent years worthy of genuine futural promise has been the sudden emergence and rapid growth of the Counterculture. In spite of the loose heterogeneity of its budding elements, the poignant thrust of its diffuse reverberations coalesces around the unshakeable core of a tirelessly repeated and consistently vociferous message: the dominant culture's total counter-productivity vis-à-vis the needful implementation of genuine human aspirations and values into society-at-large. The universal language of this Counterculture has been and will continue to be the infectious, driving dynamism of rock and roll music, and to be sure the shock-waves emanating from its vibrant center have quite literally rocked the world. If it is legitimate to speak of an ongoing cultural revolution in the West which is shaking the brittle foundations of our senescent civilization, then it hardly can be doubted that rock and roll music is not an authentic voice of this widespread and general upheaval.

    Certainly everyone caught up in it has his or her favorites in the shifting solar system of rock music, but a steady, reflective glance backwards to the tumultuous history of the 1960s and then forward to our own present brings to light an observation fraught with the utmost interpretive significance: to wit, that together with

Bob Dylan and the Beatles, the exciting lyrical, percussive energy and the radical life-style of a leering, shaggy quintet called the Rolling Stones has had and continues to have the most formative, dramatic effect on the life-orientation and world-view of dissatisfied, discontented millions who would immediately define themselves in terms of an unflinching allegiance to the developing Counterculture. It is precisely the Age of Rock which has given birth to the Rolling Stones, but what is so remarkable in all of this is a notorious dearth of intelligent commentary and written material on them, as compared to the bevy of published opinion readily available concerning Bob Dylan or the Beatles – especially when the Rolling Stones have stood out like such stellar objects of the first magnitude in the dawn of our own day. Could it well be that there is an underlying residual fear, a sneaking suspicion that the Rolling Stones embody too much what might be loosely designated 'the spirit of the times' as it were, that the black beam they cast back upon their own present is too blinding to be ever acknowledged, let alone taken with a seriousness even remotely bordering on the philosophic? We believe this to be so much the case that this book itself constitutes a dedicated, quasi-systematic attempt to rectify the currently deficient state of affairs, and thus endeavors to do at least some necessary historical justice to the existential import of the Rolling Stones, not only as a decisive rock and roll music group or as highly influential flesh-and-blood individuals, but as consequential concrete symbols, radiating prisms illuminating and typifying the 'essence' of our own times …and its involuntary dis-ease. It is precisely in this latter sense that to ask about the Rolling Stones is to raise with equal significance the fundamental issue concerning the meaning of ourselves …our very lives in the course of this convulsive epoch.

Therefore, in terms of what has been briefly sketched out in the preceding paragraphs, one dominant question continues to hauntingly animate the interpretive thrust of this book: what is the MEANING of the Rolling Stones in both an overall and underlying sense, or more pointedly, what does it MEAN TO BE a Rolling Stone? Even though it is stated in a provisionally philosophical manner, clearly this is no merely abstract, harmless question, however much it might seem so to the thoughtless and the unreceptive who characterize much of the insensitive "dead weight" of the present. For, as has already been alluded to, in its very asking is embedded much of the RADICAL UPROOTEDNESS of our own age, an age which is witnessing a planetary collision between modern man and global technology within the retrogressive context of a darkening world that is relentlessly transforming itself into a flattened-out, valueless, pure mathematical present (this exhaustive and exhausting process of 'de-spiritualization' obscenely parades itself naïvely under the euphemism of 'progress'). Because the life and personality of the now deceased Rolling Stone Brian Jones (who together with Mick Jagger and Keith Richard co-founded the group) will be the powerful magnet which draws into focus the book's manifold dimensions, it is precisely in its UNROLLING through the life-stretch of this single yet significant human being that the unordinary QUESTION pervading the book acquires the status of a productive MARK which can only be glimpsed in the form of an incisive PORTRAIT.

    If the reader will but discover some jagged fragments of his own life-history in the gathering sweep of this study, then the author feels that the book will have more than accomplished its urgent, exploratory task: an illumination of the similarity of individual fates that dovetail inexorably into a generational rubric that can be called a 'destiny.' We shall be 'on the way to wisdom' when we thinkingly accept the loosened shackles of our own fatefully binding 'destiny,' for it is assuredly only the felt resistance of these never-to-be-fully-broken chains that will allow us to dance with the tranquil yet joyous fervor of a *Zarathustra*, a *Zorba*, or a *Jumpin' Jack Flash*. This is the passionate freedom which does not so much break with and thus shatter tradition altogether, as it does re-appropriate the waiting claim of that same heritage in ever novel yet authentic ways. It is only in such a manner that we can even begin to step beyond the shrill, paralyzing nihilism of our essentially "belongingless age," the age of the Rolling Stones…[i]

> "The wandering in the direction of
> the question-worthy is not so much
> an adventure as a turning-home." – Martin Heidegger

Quiogue, Long Island   May 2, 1972

Endnote

---

[i] The carefully attentive reader will have noticed by now in *Unrolled Stone* that beneath the surface play of its language is an intentional kinship with certain ways of contemporary philosophizing. It is not essential that one be familiar with the technical philosophical underpinnings which in effect ground the book, indeed no real harm is done if one is not – but if one is, so much the better. In any case it would be a tedious exercise in fruitless pedantry to list a myriad host of relevant philosophical sources. The reader should be spared the ordeal of having to undergo a lengthy gauntlet of "merely" formal philosophical footnotes.

NOTE

It cannot be emphasized strongly enough that the *Précis* itself concisely and rigorously attempts to delineate the theoretical structure *explicitly presupposed* for UNROLLED STONE; the book, by contrast, will consciously embody an *achieved simplicity* which does away with most of the philosophical "jargon," and hence will be infinitely more readable for the interested, educable layman. Hence the sample chapter, *In Track of a Shadow*, exemplifies to a much greater degree the actual style of *Unrolled Stone* (although it must be said here that the biographical facets of this chapter have been deliberately minimalized until such time as I get to England and can personally interview the Rolling Stones themselves together with those "significant others" who can illuminate with greater depth and exactitude the Stones' historical evolution). In any case, my specific purpose is to "shoot for" those same people who have been so captivated by the writings of someone such as Hermann Hesse (or possibly R. D. Laing) – this I believe would be an enviable "happy medium."

P.S. – As of this moment (Feb. 2, 1973) R. D. Laing has a copy of the sample chapter and the Rolling Stones themselves (via their tour manager Peter Rudge) have copies of both the chapter and the *Précis*. I expect to hear from them shortly.

The Précis, How to Read It, or Not Read It: An Excursus

We freely acknowledge that the *Précis* is not an easy piece to read. Thus, with this idea in mind, we would like to make our efforts easier to understand for the average reader.

We therefore suggest three separate but related strategies to ease the complexities of the text:

1) To briefly OUTLINE and SUMMARIZE in the *Précis* the basic PHILOSOPHICAL argument "unrolled" in the somewhat lengthy *commentary (Steps 1-12), pp. 35-37*.
2) Because of its CONCRETE *philosophical significance*, that the *Précis* should be regarded as a sort of EXISTENTIAL BIBLE to which again and again one can refer back for a heightened and deeper sense of clarity and direction vis-à-vis the 'nature of our game.'
3) To admit that if the going seems to get too tough, the *Précis* threatens to sink under the cargo of its own erudition (à la Ezra Pound's *The Cantos*, his overly long poetic masterpiece). Therefore, the best advice is to *ignore* the *Précis* entirely, and flip over to *In Track of a Shadow*, the centerpiece, which is a detailed analysis of

the song "Paint It Black." The reader can then go back to the *Précis*, and go forward once again to *In Track of a Shadow* for a deepened sense of "Paint It Black" and the *entire project* of *Unrolled Stone*.

July 2015

UNDERLINED STONE:

A Portrait of THE Question As A Mark

by
L. T. Stallings
(300pp.-1972)

PRÉCIS

Title *UNROLLED STONE*:
A Portrait of *THE* Question as *A* Mark

Cover A 1966 photograph of Brian Jones (now deceased), historical originator and co-founder of the Rolling Stones, today still considered to be the greatest rock and roll group in the world. Over his face is a *semi*-transparent question mark and beneath it a timely quotation:

> "I fancy that the faces which look out at us from the past are the surest indication we have of the meaning of an epoch."
> Kenneth Clark, *Civilisation* (p. 56)

Genre ONTOLOGICAL BIOGRAPHY (which, in fact, is so radically new that there is quite literally no other work ever written with which it could be fruitfully compared). The book, in effect, is a concretely grounded, exploratory treatise on the MEANING of EXISTENCE in our time, which moves simultaneously on two interconnected levels – the PSYCHOLOGICAL (or BIOGRAPHICAL) and the PHILOSOPHICAL (or ONTOLOGICAL, ontology being the most fundamental and hence important perspective within the philosophical enterprise per se dealing with the basic features and structures of existence, viz. Being). The phenomenon of the HISTORICAL provides the vital link resulting in the reciprocal connection of the psychological and philosophical levels, thus adding force and direction to the interpretive thrust of the book.

Length Approximately 300 pages
(to be finished by October 1972).

Structure The book will consist of TEN (10) chapters, more or less of equal length (30 pages each, adding up to 300 pages). In order to heighten the "mood" of the respective chapters and the systematic tension pervading the work as a whole, each chapter will be prefaced by THREE (3) organically related quotations from the following sources:

1. The philosophical writings of Martin Heidegger (chiefly utilizing his monumental work *Being and Time*, considered to be the "sacred" systematic text of EXISTENTIAL philosophy)
2. The literary works of Hermann Hesse (who now, without a doubt, is the most widely read writer among the under 30 generation, for those both *in* and *out* of school)

3. Provocative lyrics from some of the Rolling Stones' most significant songs (e.g., "Satisfaction," "Jumpin' Jack Flash," "Sympathy for the Devil")

There will also be a Frontispiece (see p. i of this *Précis*), a Preface (see a portion of it on p. xi of this *Précis*), and as an incisive addition to the tenor of the book, a fifty-page unnumbered Introduction consisting of 100 carefully chosen photographs (two per page) depicting the life situations of Brian Jones and the other Rolling Stones. What is novel about this photographic Introduction will be the WAY it is laid out: there will be a striking aphorism or poetic stanza beneath each photograph, resulting in a mutual reinforcement of word and image (the purpose is to incarnate the philosophical EQUIVALENCE of words and images). The germ of this new technique was contained in my father's book, *The First World War: A Photographic History* (1933), where an uncannily pithy phrase or aphorism accompanied each photograph.

An example of this type of layout: a baby picture of Brian Jones, below which is said:

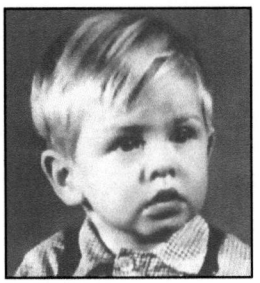
Age 3

"He was born with a gift of laughter
and a sense that the world was mad."
R. Sabatini, *Scaramouche* (p. 1)

Movement   The book, operating in close concord with its formal structure, will have a cumulative and hence comprehensive DIALECTICAL CIRCULARITY built into it which forcefully animates its direction. "Dialectical" is meant here in its original etymological or Socratic sense as a "TALKING-THROUGH" various referential contexts or positions. The book will begin with the life of Brian Jones, then will tie in his life with the growth and significance of the Rolling Stones, finally linking a definitive philosophical INTERPRETATION of the Rolling Stones with the vast yet existentially urgent question of the contemporary MEANING of EXISTENCE. After this vertical ascent to the domain of the philosophical, there will then be a backward or reverse "plunge," a gathering descent which once again returns to the life situation of Brian Jones, only this time laden with the fruitful results of philosophical encounter and assimilation.

Diagram

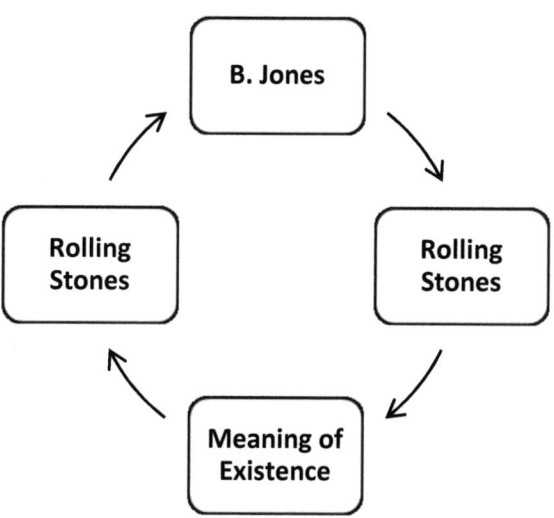

"Methods" A number of different yet interrelated analytical "engines" will be used to effectively "power" and elucidate the structural movement of the work.

Briefly, these can be and indeed must be considered in terms of their appropriate horizons of relevance:

1. PSYCHOLOGICAL (BIOGRAPHICAL) – The phenomenological psychiatry of R.D. Laing, with its radical questioning of the collective insanity euphemistically parading as "reality," and of the very distinction between sanity and madness, will be employed as a kind of MAP upon which the complex, yet intimate relation between the growth of the individual and the concentric pressures of his "world" can be delineated in "high relief" (this is particularly important in the case of Brian Jones' archetypal life and "world"). Among Laing's varied works, *The Divided Self*, *Self and Others*, and *The Politics of Experience* will be adjudged as being of special value in this regard.
2. HISTORICAL (SOCIAL) – The *Verstehen* or "Understanding" approach utilized, among others (such as the renowned pioneering sociologist Max Weber, and the profound philosophical co-founder of systematic EXISTENTIALISM, Karl Jaspers), so rewardingly by the great intellectual historian and philosopher, Ernst Cassirer. This approach, which

consciously adopts a posture of intuitive empathy, even sympathy, vis-à-vis the "matter" being studied, especially stresses the decisive significance of the "INNER," FORMATIVE FORCES upon historically consequential individuals (these in effect are "earthquake experiences," to use a Kierkegaardian expression, which are looked upon as being crucial even by the particular individual being studied, and are unraveled best in a systematic, chronological fashion). Cassirer's short, but brilliant *The Question of Jean Jacques Rousseau* will be considered as noteworthy in this respect (i.e., in terms of the lucid explication and concrete application of the *Verstehen* "method").

3. PHILOSOPHICAL (ONTOLOGICAL) – Since the underlying purpose of this book is to put "LIVING FLESH" on the ontological skeleton of DASEIN (Heidegger's term for "HUMAN BEING" in *Being and Time*, literally meaning "Being-There" in the German; see the Commentary section of this *Précis*, p. 9ff.), here is where the core of the methodological weight of the work really lies. Indeed it can be said that the philosophical validity

of the entire book stands or falls with the existential insights gleaned through the ontological analysis, and the degree to which these throw much-needed light on the concrete reality of the HUMAN CONDITION-as-such in the present historical epoch. More, much more, will be said concerning the philosophical sources of the ontological analysis in the ensuing Commentary section (particularly its essentially Nietzschean origin), but let it be briefly mentioned here that the fundamental significance of this analysis acquires its incisive shape on the scaffolding of Heidegger's *Being and Time*. More specifically, this particular type of analysis should be called "ANALYSIS of DASEIN" (DASEINSANALYSE in the German; see Medard Boss' *Psychoanalysis and Daseinsanalysis* for an excellent study of the implications of Heidegger's thinking in *Being and Time* for the twin-disciplines of psychotherapeutic theory and practice). In fact, UNROLLED STONE itself should be considered a CONCRETIZATION of the "spirit" and the essential recurring problems of *Being and Time*, albeit in a transformed sense and within a more historically "gut-level" context.

Commentary

If the exploratory task of this book seems to be grandiose, it is intended to be so. The time has come for a fruitful confrontation between "academic" philosophy and so-called "Pop" culture, now known as the "Counterculture." In a somewhat puerile sense this has already been attempted in two well-known works, T. Roszak's *The Making of a Counter-Culture* and C. Reich's *The Greening of America* (where the music of the Rolling Stones is mentioned as surpassing the energy and drive of Beethoven, and just as relevant historically in terms of its truth value), but still these books remain hopelessly mired in the bogs of philosophical naïveté, because their respective authors are simply not equipped to deal with the weighty consequences of such a confrontation (e.g., in terms of the range, scope, and depth of the problems thus opened up). (R. Meltzer's *The Aesthetics of Rock* is the other not-so-well-known work along this line, and is considered to be a "classic" in its own right, but it is really a shallow disjointed panoply of pseudo-profundities tinged with obscurities.)

Such an interpretive "collision" or confrontation between two normally disparate "worlds" admittedly will be a VIOLENT one, but such violence intrinsically belongs to *Interpretation*

ONTOLOGICALLY understood, that is to say, as a NECESSARY structure of man's existence (thus *Interpretation* is something that one "IS," not merely an activity that one "DOES"; as such, it constitutes an essential determinant of Dasein's Being-in-the-world; see Heidegger's *Being and Time* in this regard). The reason why such a collision is demanded at this time is not simply an issue of relevance, although certainly this is an important factor, and moreover one that all too much contemporary philosophizing goes at great lengths to avoid. Besides, the issue of relevance is always bound up with the CONTEMPORARY, the HISTORICAL, and thus is always subject to a bevy of opinions and perspectives. No, the necessity of such a confrontation moves within a definite philosophical framework, one in particular that can no longer be ignored by either the 'academic community' or the proverbial man-in-the-street (cf. F. Nietzsche's quip that "great philosophy problems arise in the street"). The framework that we are referring to is nothing less than that ONTOLOGICAL HORIZON which intimately surrounds, penetrates, and encompasses EVERY aspect of our daily lives in even the most personal moments; the horizon, namely of the question of the MEANING of Being-in-general or Being-as-such, to which we not only constantly relate, but concerning which we already have a PRE-VERBAL, PRE-EXPLICIT understanding or grasp (in other words, despite an implicit inability to speak adequately about it or conceptually formulate its significance). This question has become particularly crucial today, for the uncanny force and "logic" of current events have generated an overall but underlying mood of chaos, opacity, and uncertainty that is historically unprecedented and, almost without question, philosophically decisive in terms of its futural repercussions and consequences (this point will be discussed further on in this same Commentary).

For his unsurpassed efforts to re-open and ELUCIDATE in a new and most radical way (in the original Latin sense of RADIX, of "going to the ROOT" of a problem) the vast issue of the QUESTION of BEING, we openly acknowledge a tremendous philosophical indebtedness to Martin Heidegger, undoubtedly the most formidable philosophical "mind" in the world today. Although he most certainly has gone beyond it in his later writings, still his systematic masterpiece, *Being and Time* (*Sein und Zeit*, 1927), remains as one of the most influential and decisive books of this century, a veritable TIME-BOMB whose shock waves still continue to be felt in a manifold variety of creative disciplines ranging from the arts to the sciences (not "just" in the narrower region of philosophy). One of Heidegger's central points in *Being and Time* is that any philosophizing "worth its salt" MUST take with ultimate seriousness the ontological question of the MEANING of Being, and that this question itself, in order to be adequately

GROUNDED, MUST take as its NECESSARY point of departure MAN (or Dasein as he is called, meaning "Being-There," the privileged and unique PLACE or "There" where "Being" itself first IRRUPTS into existence, lighting up both man and his "world") in his CONCRETE, AVERAGE EVERYDAYNESS (as he relates to the world and "IS" for the most part day-to-day). This means that the EXISTENTIAL mode of AVERAGE EVERYDAYNESS is the KEY to any possible UNLOCKING of the question of the MEANING of Being (indeed precisely the "essence" of HUMAN BEING is his "OPENNESS-to-BEING," because he "CARES" about both the WAY in which he EXISTS and equally about its MEANING or SIGNIFICANCE in terms of the entire context of EXISTENCE itself – thus HUMAN BEING is the only being whose very Being has become and always remains an ISSUE for it). To tie Heidegger to his most illustrious predecessor, Edmund Husserl (the founder of PHENOMENOLOGY, which has since become the dominant methodological PRISM of Existential philosophy), AVERAGE EVERYDAYNESS (*Durchschnittsalltäglichkeit* in the German) is the primary "LEBENSWELT" or "LIFE-WORLD" in which man lives out the course of his life (see Husserl's "rival *Being and Time*," *The Crisis of European Sciences and Transcendental Phenomenology*, especially the noted essay on "The Origin of Geometry," pp. 353-378).

Now, to pause for a moment, what has all this "bullshit" philosophical "talk" got to do with the necessarily violent yet hopefully fruitful confrontation between "academic" philosophy and the Counterculture in general, more particularly with the Rolling Stones, and finally with the prototypal life of Brian Jones? The not so obvious answer is "PLENTY"... We have seen already that it is only by "remaining true to the earth" (see F. Nietzsche's *Thus Spoke Zarathustra*) on the plane of man's 'average everydayness' that we can even hope to adequately come to grips with and perhaps illuminate the issue of Being, which today has reached the proportions of a planetary CRISIS for man-as-such (KRISIS in the fundamental Greek sense of the term means a "BREAK"). Indeed, it is no accident that a crucial reason for the increasing popularity of the philosophical writings of the remarkable 19th century German thinker, Friedrich Nietzsche, as well as the EXISTENTIAL seriousness with which they are taken (e.g., Hermann Hesse has openly acknowledged that Nietzsche was his "spiritual" father), is precisely their illuminative power regarding the raison d'être for this same CRISIS or "BREAK," together with the courageous resoluteness Nietzsche as an "untimely" thinker displayed in unfalteringly forging ahead into an existential VOID or ABYSS, whose eddying suction irresistibly tugs at our very lives today with an ever-gathering momentum (to this extent, it is not merely as a shallow exercise in pedantry that Mick Jagger's "spiritual Siamese-twin," Turner, cryptically quotes Nietzsche in the haunting film *Performance* when he utters: "Nothing is true, everything is permitted..."). Moreover, it might well be said that the inner dynamism of UNROLLED STONE itself is continuously energized by the animating core of an essentially Nietzschean vision or perspective: namely, acceptance of the historical fact that "GOD IS DEAD," which is a poignant religious metaphor icily reflecting the "nature" of this CRISIS – to wit, that the heretofore apodictic provenance of VALUES has been irrevocably "BROKEN" in our time, resulting in a concomitant "BREAK" in MAN'S SELF-UNDERSTANDING, in TRADITION, in HISTORY, in TIME, in "REALITY-itself" (Nietzsche's two most significant works, *Thus Spoke Zarathustra* and *The Will to Power*, are considered to be particularly indispensable in being supremely revelatory of his own philosophical vistas and their boundless horizons).

After the much talked-about "KEHRE" or "REVERSAL" in his thinking, Heidegger himself has "gotten away" from the phenomenon of 'average everydayness' because, in a sense, the strictness of his own thinking has demanded it. Heidegger's thought itself "broke down" in the attempt to move from the 'average everydayness' of human *being* TO the historical "nature" of *Being-itself*, and as a result he has come to rethink the ontological question of Being FROM the perspective of Being-

ITSELF (that is to say he now inquires as to the WAYS in which Being "comes" to man). Since this means that he has had to concentrate on those exceptional, gifted, receptive "antennae of the race," so to speak, who initially hear the call of Being and subsequently are able to express its meaning to mankind-at-large in the form of great works of art, philosophy, acts of statesmanship, and religious prophecy, Heidegger has had to "ignore," relatively speaking, the dimension of man's 'average everydayness' in order to pursue faithfully the course of his own thinking. However, it must be said that even Heidegger's later thinking still remains rooted in 'average everydayness' in a double sense: (1) in so far as an understanding of Heidegger's later thought presupposes a comprehension of his earlier thinking of *Being and Time*; (2) in the sense that the presence of man's everydayness can be sensed or "felt" by the sensitive reader in Heidegger's later efforts, although this is a silent, unexplicitated presence (it is more often the wondrous, evocative everydayness of inexhaustible THINGS and not of Dasein or man). Thus we see that Heidegger has become Nietzschean to the extent that he has focused much of his own philosophical force on the exceptional, creative individuals so vital in their DISCLOSIVE power vis-à-vis the historical DESTINY of Being.

We, however, wish to TARRY longer in that DECISIVE mode of man's 'average everydayness' so constitutive of the HUMAN CONDITION in toto, for in terms of the HERMENEUTIC perspective of the EFFECTIVELY-HISTORICAL CONSCIOUSNESS ("WIRKUNGSGESCHICHTLICHES BEWUSSTSEIN") – see H.-G. Gadamer's *Truth and Method* (*Wahrheit und Methode*), it is precisely HERE where the real significance of the Counterculture lies. (HERMENEUTICS actually is a specific philosophical "attitude or "stance" developed by Heidegger and more recently, by Gadamer; it is virtually a synonym for "Interpretation ONTOLOGICALLY understood," to which reference has already been made at the beginning of this Commentary. It additionally has much in common with the notion of "ANALYSIS of DASEIN," also referred to in the section entitled "Methods" in this *Précis*. Hermeneutics derives from the original Greek word "HERMENEUEIN," meaning to "INTERPRET" or "REVEAL," and more concretely to the mythical HERMES, or MERCURY in Roman mythology, who, as the MESSENGER of the gods and MEDIATOR, made intelligible the enigmatic ways of the gods to men). Our thesis is that the VALUES, music, art, politics, life-style, etc., of the Counterculture already have been and will continue to be 'historically-effective' on the 'average everydayness' of Dasein, which constitutes his most habitual 'life-world.' This is even more apparent if we view this "HAPPENING" (in German

GESCHICHTE or "HISTORY" has a close etymological kinship with the verb GESCHEHEN, "TO HAPPEN") in terms of a GENERATIONAL matrix. As a result, we can see that the Counterculture has already transformed essential aspects of the VITAL phenomenon of 'average everydayness.' Such a transformation thus can only be called "REVOLUTIONARY," however much such a de facto decisive event appears to be superficial or transitory at first glance.

Nonetheless, the greatest danger today facing the authentic growth of the Counterculture is truly an ominous one: loss of its newly-found rootedness and "spiritual" autonomy to the extent that it becomes TRIVIALIZED as a genuine cultural force (H. Marcuse's *One Dimensional Man* should be cited here, regarding the parasitic, coercive power of the dominant "Culture" or "Establishment"). The renowned German historian Oswald Spengler inadvertently has depicted in a most striking fashion precisely the DILEMMA of the Counterculture when, in a reference to the "development" of Arabic-Magian culture upon the bedrock of Classical Antiquity, he muses:

> "By the term 'historical pseudomorphosis' I propose to designate those cases in which an older alien Culture lies so massively over the land that a young Culture, born in this land, cannot get its breath and fails not

> only to achieve pure and specific expression forms, but even to develop fully its own self-consciousness. All that wells up from the depths of the young soul is cast into the old molds, young feelings stiffen in senile works, and instead of rearing itself up in its own creative power, it can only hate the distant power with a hate that grows to be monstrous."
>
> *Decline of the West* (p. 268, Abridged edition)

Needless to say, UNROLLED STONE itself specifically attempts to significantly offset this real danger by a simultaneous "DEEPENING" of "academic" philosophy and an "ELEVATION" of the Counterculture, the result of which will be a cross-fertilization and reciprocal radicalization of both (concretely, of course, this will be accomplished through an incisive HERMENEUTICS of the Rolling Stones and the paradigmatic life of Brian Jones).

Quite obviously, there exists an intimate connection between the Rolling Stones (and hence Brian Jones) and the budding Counterculture, in fact one that is decisive in a sense that goes far beyond the matrix of the latter. Taking as a clue for a subtle point of departure a profound insight of the highly idiosyncratic, yet famous, recent Austrian-born philosopher Ludwig Wittgenstein in his almost legendary final work, *Philosophical Investigations* (*Philosophische Untersuchungen*): an implicit, indissoluble BOND exists between a particular LANGUAGE GAME and its appropriate FORM of LIFE (LEBENSFORM), and moreover the former is only understandable in terms of the latter (thus, as can be readily perceived, Wittgenstein's delineation of the LANGUAGE GAME-FORM OF LIFE reciprocity represents a helpful *dichotomization* of the Heideggerian notion of AVERAGE EVERYDAYNESS and the related Husserlian concept of the LIFE-WORLD). Since rock and roll music in general is without a doubt the most universally valid ARTICULATION of that FORM of LIFE commonly known as the Counterculture (i.e., it IS its "LANGUAGE" and in this sense, moreover, perhaps the most UNIVERSAL LANGUAGE GAME in the world today, one having an undeniably GENERATIONAL significance), this music has become, not surprisingly, the symbolic KEYSTONE in the existential ARCH of the Counterculture-as-such (actually, in terms of its TOTAL import, this same music unintentionally *transcends* the sphere of the Counterculture). Historically, of course, rock and roll music evolved out of the Black *sub*-or-*counter*-culture (itself the articulation of collective Black experience in America), and more specifically out of the Black experience within a concrete sociological context of rapid URBANIZATION, this being a demographic result of the growing dominance of TECHNOLOGY and the concomitant demands of ORGANIZATION in the world at large (in this regard, see two interesting works: L. Jones' *Blues People*, and C. Gillett's

The Sound of the City). Consequently, rock and roll music being the "LANGUAGE" of the Counterculture (and thus the "LANGUAGE" of GENERATIONAL "REVOLT" on the part of YOUTH in a world-wide sense), the important question must now be asked: which rock and roll group best typifies both the "essence" of the music and the most "AUTHENTIC" WAY or FORM of LIFE (cf. Wittgenstein's idea of LEBENSFORM here) inextricably bound up with it? The answer is quite simply, "the Rolling Stones!"

This writer himself long ago, upon seeing a Rolling Stones' concert after just returning "from some time in Africa and Asia with the Peace Corps, voiced the opinion that the Stones and their ilk are a social revolution which may have as much effect as Karl Marx" (*Honolulu Star-Bulletin*, July 29, 1966, p. B-4). Even staid *Newsweek* magazine, in a recent cover article on "The Future of Rock" (January 4, 1971, pp. 44-48) said of them:

> "…Their long popularity, their subtly subversive music, their much-publicized yet still myth-shrouded life-style and their relation to the revolutionary fervor marking the end of the '60s offer a prismatic view of a cultural phenomenon that has literally rocked the world.
>
> "…Seldom understated, the Stones precipitated a turned-on frenzy and unleashed a submerged

rebelliousness in both boys and girls as no other group did. Where the carefully groomed Beatles came across in the beginning as kicky, sassy boys next door to be swooned over by crush-ridden teeny-boppers, Jagger and the Stones immediately homed in on the deeper, fugitive malaise bubbling in the more sophisticated youth of both sexes." (p.45)

In addition, it can be no mere accident that the two major publications of the Counterculture in the United States today are entitled *Rolling Stone* and *Crawdaddy* (the latter being the name of a now legendary club in the Richmond suburb of London where the Rolling Stones began their meteoric rise back in February 1963). The upshot of all this is that it would seem we have an "airtight" case: (1) rock and roll music is the universal "LANGUAGE" of the Counterculture; and (2) the Rolling Stones concretely symbolize the "essence" of this "LANGUAGE" together with a "summing-up" of that "FORM OF LIFE" (LEBENSFORM) most clearly associated with it. In fact, according to that same Newsweek article already cited: "No group better illustrates rock's apocalyptic rise and blossoming sociopolitical accouterments…" (p. 45). This justifies Andrew Loog Oldham's seemingly outrageous liner-notes to their first record-album (released May 29th, 1964), where he prophetically remarks: "The Rolling Stones are more than just a group, they are a WAY of LIFE" (this writer's emphasis).

However, a major point to be constantly stressed in the Hermeneutic sweep of this book is that it would be drastically shortsighted to confine the significance of the Rolling Stones simply to the symbolic vanguard of the Counterculture, important though this be in its own right. The cultural MYOPIA of much contemporary "philosophizing" has been notorious in matters of this sort, when, all too often, its initial judgment of irrelevancy concerning the emergence of new phenomena outside of the usual crystalline narrowness of its own sphere has really been a sign of its own historical AGORAPHOBIA. To begin with, the very name of the group is a profound poetic metaphor, a *cipher* (cf. K. Jaspers here) pregnant with immense PHILOSOPHICAL significance, for it immediately suggests, indeed points to a depth of UPROOTEDNESS, UNEASY 'FREEDOM,' ALIENATION, RESTLESSNESS, …of HOMELESSNESS that inexorably has become today a WORLD-DESTINY valid for MAN-AS-SUCH (concretely, it will be the task of UNROLLED STONE to delineate precisely WHY this is compellingly the case not merely for the Rolling Stones and hence Brian Jones, but to what extent we have all become "Rolling Stones"). Moreover, the entire thematic edifice of their "gut-level" music not only rises up out of, authentically "mirrors," and doggedly returns to the SEARCHING UNCERTAINTY of their DAILY LIVES with an almost unmatched intensity (cf. Heidegger's notion of AVERAGE EVERYDAYNESS and Husserl's concept of the LIFE-WORLD here), but it unflinchingly attests to the stark PHILOSOPHICAL TRUTH implied by their haunting name: viz. a DISQUIETING ROOTLESSNES is the 'normal' condition of contemporary man, whose life is an *anxious* shuttling between the Scylla of *sensual abandon* and the Charybdis of *"gnawing" boredom*. "I CAN'T GET NO SATISFACTION" is not merely a song by the Rolling Stones with "heavy" metaphysical 'roots' in Hegel (whose brilliant *Phenomenology of Spirit* shows that NEGATIVITY is the indispensable "driving power" in the dialectic of human consciousness), but more fundamentally, it is the ANSWERLESS Faustian CRY of an entire historical epoch, where "NOTHINGNESS lies like a worm coiled-up in the heart of Being" (see J.P. Sartre's *Being and Nothingness*). Likewise, "Sympathy for the Devil" is only superficially the musical incarnation of a diabolical discourse; in reality it is an explicit recognition of the TRAGIC, unavoidable BRUTALITY embedded within the HISTORICAL PROCESS itself …even an *active* acceptance of it (after seeing Mick Jagger leeringly sing the chilling line "Stuck around St. Petersburg when I saw it was time for a change; killed the Tsar and his ministers, Anastasia screamed in vain…" a vivid metaphor of Max Weber comes to mind: world history resembles a street paved by the devil with destroyed values). Only the enveloping "DOME" of a COSMIC "YES" sung in "Jumpin Jack Flash" ("…But it's ALL-L-L RIGHT, in fact it's a GAS!!") can give birth to the "EARTHY-LAUGH" needed to surmount the sheer EXISTENTIAL HORROR of planetary homelessness as well as of the sense-less brutality inherent in historical time (cf. Hesse's *Steppenwolf* and Nikos Kazantzakis' *Zorba The Greek* here). Perhaps this is the "REAL" MEANING of the Rolling Stones expressed in a PHILOSOPHICAL fashion, but who knows? ..It must be "UNROLLED"…

Such an intrinsic connection between the symbolic quality of the Rolling Stones' very name and the philosophical truth delineated by the implicit VALUES contained within the body of their music and intimately related WAY of LIFE cannot be sloughed off as solely accidental, without losing sight of their already alluded-to EFFECTIVELY-HISTORICAL and TRANSFORMATIVE impact upon the very style and substance of the present age (most particularly the under-30 generation). It must be realized that the name "Rolling Stones" derives from a 1950 Muddy Waters rhythm and blues song, "Rollin' Stone" (which is indicative of the leitmotif of rootless WANDERING and TRANSIENCY permeating the bulk of American Black music – see P. Oliver's magnificent work, *The*

Meaning of the Blues, in this regard). Indeed, this very name was consciously CHOSEN out of a feeling of cultural indebtedness and belongingness to the HERITAGE of Black music, as well as out of an implicit recognition of the EXISTENTIALLY ROOTLESS CONDITION of modern man-as-such (concerning which the American Black man is a historical PRECURSOR). "Rolling Stones" is not only a philosophical cipher pregnant with disclosive power, but also a striking poetic metaphor speaking directly to an entire generation and its surrounding historical "world" about the REAL CONDITIONS of its own "GUT-LEVEL" EXISTENCE (probably this was the EMOTIONAL "LEVER" that so MOVINGLY AFFECTED the three co-founders of the group back in 1962, viz. Mick Jagger, Brian Jones, and Keith Richard). In short, "Rollin' Stone," is, in the words of R. Gordon, "a song about power, about rootlessness – and ruthless independence" (*Muddy Waters*, p. 104).

In the process of *Hermeneutically* explicitating the growth and significance of the Rolling Stones, the crucial ARCHETYPAL position of their late guitarist, Brian Jones, must not be overlooked, so instrumental was he in the LAYING-DOWN of the group's initial musical orientation, its concomitant existential ATTITUDES and VALUES, and its RADICALLY-NOVEL LIFE-STYLE and PUBLIC "IMAGE" (all of which were irritatingly defiant of and abrasive to conventional standards of bourgeois propriety). The CENTRALITY of Jones' ROLE is *not*, repeat, is NOT based upon the mere arbitrariness of this writer's personal preference, but has been noted even by the highly-regarded *Rolling Stone* magazine. Specifically, in a special cover article of the August 9th, 1969 issue commenting upon his accidental death of July 2nd in that same year (disturbingly headlined "Brian Jones: Sympathy for the Devil"), *Rolling Stone* said:

> "If Keith Richard and Mick Jagger were the mind and body of the Rolling Stones, Brian Jones, standing most of the time in the shadows, was clearly the soul.
>
> "Brian, in with Keith and Mick from the earliest – when the Stones were largely an (sic!) R&B discussion group meeting in a Soho pub – was labeled the quietest, the moodiest of the group. But he was in fact the most vocal to the press, angrily and sharply defending the Stones' then-radical style of music, their appearance, their politics, and their whole style of life.
>
> "…He was a Rolling Stone before he joined in 1962, and he led the life of a true Rolling Stone from 1963 to 1969." (p.1)

In an additional article in the same issue, Greil Marcus ventures:

"Jones was perhaps more of a Rolling Stone than any of the others. What the Stones as a group sang about, what Jagger and Richard wrote about, Jones did, and he did it right out in public, and he got caught, and he looked the part. ... that was Brian Jones. A true rake. He wasn't acting out the Stones' music, he just happened to BE the Stones' music, and that was one reason why you know the Stones always mean it, why you know they aren't sitting around thinking up clever ideas that might make a good song – it was always valid …and Jones was the reason, part of the reason …" (p.6)

Actually, what is so moving and seductive here about Marcus' timely remarks on Brian Jones is not that they are solely an implicit panegyric couched in a matter-of-fact style proper to good journalism, but rather they point to something more profoundly fundamental, yet for all that still shimmeringly ENIGMATIC – something already "UNDERSTOOD" EXISTENTIALLY, yet almost DEFYINGLY RESISTANT to adequate "Interpretation" or THEMATIZATION (Hermeneutics itself is characterized by an ONTOLOGICAL alternation between "UNDERSTANDING" and "Interpretation"; this means that the chief function of "Interpretation" is a "WORKING-OUT," a "MAKING-EXPLICIT" of what is already within the range of EXISTENTIAL "UNDERSTANDING" or human awareness, which is "EMOTIONALLY" REAL but nevertheless PRE-ARTICULATE or PRE-THEMATIC: see Heidegger's *Being and Time* and Gadamer's *Wahrheit und Methode* in this regard). This 'something more profoundly fundamental' touches us to the very quick when he says that Brian Jones "wasn't acting out the Stones' music, he just happened to BE the Stones' music..." – indeed, this comment equally excites and disturbs the attuned reader. Since an emotional ambivalence of this sort is almost always indicative of something essential "HAPPENING" in the hidden recesses of our own individual Being (our Dasein as it were) it must not be lightly skipped over. For what does it MEAN 'to BE the Stones' music'? Whatever that is, the "answer" is necessarily an EXISTENTIAL and not a musical one (the "answer" must throw light on the more primordial question considered to be absolutely crucial in the interpretive thrust of UNROLLED STONE: viz. 'What does it mean to BE a Rolling Stone,' or in a more provisional Kantian language – 'What are the CONDITIONS for the POSSIBILITY of a Rolling Stone'? see the Preface in this Précis). Furthermore, to BE this type of music necessarily means to BE what it is ABOUT (Wittgenstein's LANGUAGE GAME-FORM of LIFE reciprocity should be fruitfully recalled here). Thus, one of the REVOLUTIONARY features of the Rolling Stones' music has been its persistent, uncompromising coming-to-grips-with the normally UNPALATABLE "FACTS" of DAILY LIFE (cf. Heidegger's

'AVERAGE EVERYDAYNESS' and Husserl's 'LIFE-WORLD' here), its so-called "DARK" SIDE. Consequently, themes such as EXISTENTIAL ANXIETY, MENTAL DISINTEGRATION, SEXUAL EXPLOITATION, and SENSUAL IMMERSION have been common facets of this "DARK" SIDE in their music, all of which are ultimately guided by an underlying sense of artistic INTEGRITY, existential TRUTHFULNESS, and an over-all PENCHANT for a greater FREEDOM laced with a sense of HUMOR which itself is indicative of increasing awareness (in spite of the concomitant RISKS, even the personal threat of COLLAPSE, of "SHIPWRECK," that this latter entails). All of this and then some is what Brian Jones 'happened to BE,' and it is perhaps in this light that Rolling Stone magazine dubbed him 'clearly the soul' of the Rolling Stones (however, this writer should like to add here that the near-legendary Mick Jagger and Keith Richard are *not* thereby diminished in stature or import; historically, Jagger, Jones, and Richard always have been considered to be the *inner core* of the group – of course now that Jones is dead, Jagger has become, so to speak, the 'soul' of the Rolling Stones). To BE the Rolling Stones' music is to be MORE THAN a Rolling Stone MUSICALLY, it is to BE a 'Rolling Stone' ONTOLOGICALLY (i.e., as the RADICALIZATION of an essential tendency of BEING, or EXISTENCE, appropriate to a HISTORICAL EPOCH shot through with HOMELESSNESS as a WORLD-DESTINY).

It would be a complete *mis*-understanding of the interpretive sweep of UNROLLED STONE to think that what is intended here is really the disguised HAGIOGRAPHY of a dead "pop" star clothed in the insulated trappings of philosophical "legitimacy." Rather, as should be apparent from the subtitle of this book, 'A Portrait of *THE* Question as *A* Mark,' this writer has quite different "fish to fry." This subtitle obviously punningly recalls James Joyce's *A Portrait of the Artist as a Young Man* (and to this extent there are definite psychological similarities between the Rolling Stones in general as young artists, Brian Jones in particular, and Joyce's Stephen Dedalus), but more importantly it immediately suggests a famous philosophical observation by Nietzsche to the effect that, now that 'God is dead' HISTORICALLY in our time, MAN-AS-SUCH has become "a QUESTION-MARK caught between two NOTHINGS (i.e., the PAST and the FUTURE)." Since man himself now has become his own greatest question, this means that the very MEANING of EXISTENCE obtrusively emerges as historically urgent in an EXISTENTIAL manner, as well as being ONTOLOGICALLY necessary in a strictly PHILOSOPHICAL sense. However, this question is so vast in scope and depth that it must be concretely MARKED and UNROLLED in a penetrating fashion through the medium of HERMENEUTICS (where to "Interpret" means to MAKE-EXPLICIT, or "UNROLL").

Thus, the upshot of this is that Brian Jones (together with the Rolling Stones as a group) is made in UNROLLED STONE the ONTOLOGICAL FOCAL POINT, the PIVOT as it were, of an all-embracing PHILOSOPHICAL problem, THE QUESTION of the MEANING of EXISTENCE (BEING) in our time. Brian Jones is the STONE who must be "UNROLLED" (i.e., Hermeneutically) because as a PERSONIFICATION of the Rolling Stones (who themselves are CONCRETE ONTOLOGICAL SYMBOLS for HOMELESSNESS-become-a-WORLD-DESTINY), he is a 'historically effective' MARK of the QUESTION of EXISTENCE. Hence, it is not for nothing that there will be *semi*-transparent QUESTION-MARK over his face on the cover of UNROLLED STONE (*semi*-transparent because of the INCOMPLETENESS intrinsically belonging to all investigative activity, whether directed towards oneself, other-selves, or the "world"). It is in this PHILOSOPHICAL sense that Brian Jones' life (and position vis-à-vis the Rolling Stones) should be referred to as 'archetypal,' 'prototypal,' or 'paradigmatic.'

In order that Brian Jones (and the Rolling Stones) as Hermeneutic "TARGETS" do not disappear under the sheer weight of the ensuing philosophical problematic, UNROLLED STONE is not simply an ontological MARK of the question of Existence, but EQUALLY a BIOGRAPHICAL PORTRAIT of this same question (thus the term 'ONTOLOGICAL BIOGRAPHY' for the book's unique, unusually radical genre). Just as Nietzsche's thought will be the inner core guiding the ontological part of this book, so the LIFE and PERSONALITY of the 19th century French "REBEL" poet, Arthur Rimbaud, will be the powerful magnet which draws into FOCUS the book's BIOGRAPHICAL dimensions sharply enough for a PORTRAIT. In an outstanding study of him by the well-known writer Henry Miller, *The Time of the Assassins* its title, Miller says warningly: "…I think there are many Rimbauds in this world and that their number will increase with time. I think the Rimbaud type will displace, in the world to come, the Hamlet type and the Faustian type …Until the old world dies out utterly, the 'abnormal' individual will tend more and more to be the norm" (p. 6). As YOUNG, "OUTCASTE" ARTISTS, Rimbaud, Brian Jones, and the life-situations of the Rolling Stones evidently have much in common (see Rimbaud's "BATTLE-CRY" to poets which is the Frontispiece in this Précis). Not only did Rimbaud have his Harar (Ethiopia) and Jones his Joujouka (Morocco), but Rimbaud asked for extreme unction on a gangrene-ridden deathbed (after writing 'Death to God!' in chalk on a church-wall as a youth), and Jones privately confessed – "I wish I never left home" – just months before his tragic death in a swimming-pool (after choosing in his youth to be a 'Rolling Stone'). UNROLLED STONE will thus consider Brian Jones and the other Rolling Stones to be

BIOGRAPHICALLY Rimbaud-types in its attempt to retain the PERSONAL and the SUBJECTIVELY "STRIKING" in its philosophical musings and ruminations (this will give a more "GUT-LEVEL" thrust to the book).

Recalling the diagram of DIALECTICAL CIRCULARITY (see p. 4 of this *Précis*) characterizing the gathering movement of UNROLLED STONE, it must be remembered that this very Commentary section itself of the *Précis* STARTS from a completely OPPOSITE point of DEPARTURE than will the book. In other words, the Commentary began from the *Meaning of Existence*-pole of the CIRCLE and moved in a CLOCKWISE, PHILOSOPHICAL ARC through the Rolling Stones to the LIFE of Brian Jones; UNROLLED STONE, on the other hand, will BEGIN with the LIFE of Brian Jones, work in a like CLOCKWISE direction through the Rolling Stones to the *Meaning of Existence*-pole, thence returning to the Rolling Stones, and finally to Brian Jones again (the movement of the book from Brian Jones and the Rolling Stones to the *Meaning of Existence*-pole will be a predominantly BIOGRAPHICAL PORTRAIT, whereas the backward 'plunge' from there once more to the Rolling Stones and the LIFE-SITUATION of Brian Jones will be chiefly an ONTOLOGICAL INTERROGATION of THE QUESTION of Existence at its appropriate levels). Furthermore, it must be kept in mind that this DIALECTICAL

CIRCULARITY is simultaneously a HERMENEUTIC one, and therefore indefinitely REPEATABLE, in as much as the ONTOLOGICAL alternation between "existential" understanding and thematic interpretation typifying Hermeneutics (see p. 27 of this *Précis*) is a recurring condition bound-up with the very course of Human Existence-as-such (Dasein). Consequently, it is possible to express the repeatable circularity of the Hermeneutic or "Analysis of Dasein" (see p. 8 of this *Précis*) STRATEGY of UNROLLED STONE in the following, somewhat sketchy manner:

1. To *Understand* Brian Jones is to *Interpret* the Rolling Stones.
2. To *Understand* the Rolling Stones is to *Interpret* rock and roll music.
3. To *Understand* rock and roll music is to *Interpret* the Counterculture (i.e., this music is its unifying "Language").
4. To *Understand* the Counterculture is to *Interpret* 'average everydayness.'
5. To *Understand* 'average everydayness' is to *Interpret* THE QUESTION of the *Meaning of Existence*.
6. To *Understand* THE QUESTION of the *Meaning of Existence* is to *Interpret* Brian Jones ... (Repeat)

1. To *Understand* Brian Jones is to *Interpret* the Rolling Stones ...etc.

By way of conclusion, it would now be proper to briefly OUTLINE the basic PHILOSOPHICAL argument "unrolled" in the somewhat lengthy *Commentary*:

1. The Question of Being is the primordial philosophical framework decisive for life and thought (Heidegger's *Being and Time*, but actually with 'forgotten' historical roots in Aristotle's *Metaphysics*).
2. With the historical 'death of God' (Nietzsche), man-as-such lives in a situation of PERMANENT CRISIS (he is a 'Question-Mark caught between two NOTHINGS'), and the philosophical Question of Being becomes EXISTENTIALLY paramount.
3. The Question of Being itself must be adequately grounded in the "GUT-LEVEL" context of 'average everydayness' (Heidegger, but also cf. Husserl's concept of the 'life-world' here).
4. 'Average everydayness' has been and is being historically transformed by the Counterculture (cf. Gadamer's notion of the 'effectively-historical consciousness').

5. Consequently, there must be a collision between 'academic' philosophy and the Counterculture if philosophy itself is to better understand 'average everydayness,' which is the KEY to the UNLOCKING of the Question of Being. Two pragmatically relevant reasons for this confrontation are:
    a. The danger of the increasing irrelevancy and isolation of philosophy from LIFE (i.e., its HISTORICAL AGORAPHOBIA).
    b. The danger of the trivialization and historical death of the Counterculture without its having understood itself EXPLICITLY (i.e., Interpreted itself).
6. Philosophy should view the Counterculture as consisting of a 'form of life' as well as a 'language game' (Wittgenstein).
7. Rock and roll music is the essential "Language" of the Counterculture, having an almost universal appeal (it is the KEYSTONE in the existential ARCH of the Counterculture).
8. The Rolling Stones are the "essence" of rock and roll music and therefore the embodiment of the "Language" of the Counterculture (the Age of Rock has given birth to the Stones who Roll!).

9. The Rolling Stones also best typify the 'form of life' of the Counterculture because there is little if any difference between what their music is ABOUT and who they ARE (i.e., they are a 'WAY of LIFE').
10. As a 'WAY of LIFE' the Rolling Stones are a philosophical cipher and a poetic metaphor for HOMELESSNESS-become-a-WORLD-DESTINY, which is an ONTOLOGICAL truth with 'roots' in Nietzsche, as well as a BIOGRAPHICAL life-situation with an exemplary historical origin in Rimbaud.
11. Historically, the now-dead Brian Jones is a PERSONIFICATION of what it means to be a 'Rolling Stone' MUSICALLY, as a 'WAY of LIFE,' and hence ONTOLOGICALLY.
12. Ergo philosophy must encounter Brian Jones and the Rolling Stones if it is to concretely explicitate ever more radically the crucial issues facing it in the above-reasons 1 through 5.

In hopefully combining the EXISTENTIAL URGENCY of Hesse's *Steppenwolf* and the METAPHYSICAL SUBTLETY of Spengler's *Decline of the West*, UNROLLED STONE will strenuously pursue the all-embracing problem of HOMELESSNESS as it is ONTOLOGICALLY concretized in the BIOGRAPHICAL life-situation of the Rolling Stones (especially Brian Jones). Indeed, it is precisely in this respect that the book acquires a critical importance, for according to writer Susan Sontag, "Most serious thought in our time struggles with the feeling of homelessness" (see her fascinating short essay on the renowned French anthropologist, Claude Levi-Strauss, entitled "The Anthropologist as Hero"). Moreover, in an age when a directionless NIHILISM (the COLLAPSE of VALUES implied by the historical 'death of God') is rapidly becoming the invisible UPROOTING force propelling the course of the world, there is a sneaking suspicion operative in UNROLLED STONE that to pose the question of HOMELESSNESS in the "gut-level" form of 'What does it MEAN to BE a ROLLING STONE?' is synonymous with asking 'What does it MEAN to BE?' (to this degree is UNROLLED STONE a 'CONCRETIZATION' of Heidegger's *Being and Time*). Hence, in their capacity as RADIATING PRISMS illuminating much of the NOTHINGNESS at the bottom of our time, are not the Rolling Stones themselves also victimized by it? In this very question is involved the ability of stepping BEYOND the opaque horizon of NIHILISM, thus making a Hermeneutics of the Rolling Stones also a HISTORICAL REFLECTION on the 'dizzying' problem of NIHILISM. One is reminded here not only of the highly personal, tragic examples of Rimbaud and Nietzsche, but more recently of Brian Jones himself. To cite a particularly poignant line from a newly-released song by the late Jim Morrison of the Doors, who was likewise a mortal 'victim' of this 'uncanny' process:

> "You're all alone…
> Like a Rolling Stone…
> Like Brian Jones…
> On a tightrope ride…"
> ('Tightrope Ride')

Consequently, an overpowering, almost irrefutable justification of the existential need, historical relevance, and philosophical necessity for a book such as UNROLLED STONE seems to have been more than adequately made in this *Précis*…

FINIS

The Stones in the Park

"Alright! Ok now listen, will you just cool it for a minute 'cos I really would like to say sommit for Brian. I'd really dig it if you would be with us while I do it. I really don't know how to do this kind of thing, but I'm goin' to try. I'd like to say a few words that I feel about Brian and I'm sure you do and what we feel about him just going when we didn't expect him to… Ah you going to be quiet or not? I'm going to say something written by Shelley."
- Mick

> *Peace, peace! he is not dead, he doth not sleep –*
> *He hath awakened from the dream of life –*
> *'Tis we, who lost in stormy visions, keep*
> *With phantoms an unprofitable strife,*
> *And in mad trance, strike with our spirit's knife*
> *Invulnerable nothings. – We decay*
> *Like corpses in a charnel; fear and grief*
> *Convulse us and consume us day by day,*
> *And cold hopes swarm like worms within our living clay.*
> *The One remains, the many change and pass;*
> *Heaven's light forever shines, Earth's shadows fly;*
> *Life, like a dome of many-coloured glass,*
> *Stains the white radiance of Eternity,*
> *Until Death tramples it to fragments. – Die,*
> *If thou wouldst be with that which thou dost seek!*
> *Follow where all is fled!*
>
> *Adonais by Percy Bysshe Shelley (1792-1822)*

"He will be somewhat TABOO
in his village the rest of his life."

   Brion Gysin in Joujouka

Scapegoat

Stonely ..stonely ..rolling ..
His tangled life-rope stretches, spirals ..
    from gingerbread Cheltenham houses
    to the Dionysian haze of Joujouka piping ..
Rolling ..rolling ..rolling ...

Fishchild face-down in a concrete womb of water,
Rootless in life, uprooted in death -
    Brian Jones, we shall not forget you -
Your stone now gathered with the green moss of memory,
You are sheltered from the panic of groundless life
    in the rootedness of our templed hearts.

The mark of your life is a hushed question ..
Which must resound throughout ..
    the reverberating tunnels of our being,
If we are to lift and tie its eddying sense
To the Gordian knot, EXISTENCE-as-such
    in the rippling Rimbaudic tail-fire ..
That is the arcing comet of our untethered times.

O the chandala, the masked chandala of Cheltenham -
    outcaste of the cast-outs -
Has slipped back into ..
    the addled "marshes of the West" ...
Faithless chaos was his darkling god,
Such a world-destiny has homelessness become ....

                                                                 —L.J. Stallings

Edvard Munch, *The Scream*, 1895

"Dread reveals Nothing." – M. Heidegger

"There is nothing to be afraid of. Nothing. Exactly." – R.D. Laing

"Maybe then I'll fade away
And not have to face the facts
It's not easy facing up
When your whole world is black."
– M. Jagger / K. Richard

In Track of a Shadow

In previous chapters we have tried to develop with sufficient depth, clarity, and rigor what might be designated the existential significance of the Rolling Stones, to probe the concrete truth-claim that the intertwining of their music and their lives puts to each one of us, especially if we have been moved by their presence on the contemporary scene. Furthermore, this comprehensive attempt to radically interpret the Stones, to regard them as nothing less than the soundtrack of the times, has been consistently guided from its inception by the enigmatic life of the late Brian Jones, and as we shall see in this chapter, not without good reasons. For Jones' life casts a giant shadow across the torturous path of the Rolling Stones, a shadow unquestionably present and beckoning, yet fleeting and dark with mystery. Nevertheless this shadow must be tracked down if we are to thematically track the sound of the Stones, as it remains to be shown in later chapters precisely why and how Brian's shadow is itself adumbrated by the horizon of a more momentous question – a question already there, albeit cryptically, in the very subtitle of this book. Then will be disclosed the normally invisible philosophical axis around which the inexhaustible musical universe of the Rolling Stones churns resolutely with a Dionysian frenzy.

Let us recall that, like the five individual yet perfectly coordinated fingers on the same groping hand,[i] from the first the Stones had instinctively reached back, digging deep into archaic and rural blues styles, in order to fully grasp the meaning of American black music. Viewed from this perspective, Mick Jagger's youthful retort to his father's derogatory labeling of this music as "jungle music" – that it had been the most real thing he had ever known – becomes not only perfectly understandable, but instantly akin to the raw emotional undercurrent fusing Mick with the rest of the group. It has been and continues to be the mesmerizing power of blues music which so enchanted the Rolling Stones. Therefore, it is no surprise that the Stones began as a blues-oriented group out of a firm desire to sink their musical roots into the traditional subsoil of a gut-level blues idiom, an idiom to which by birth, though plainly not by temperament, they were so alien. Indeed this is why they keenly felt that mimesis, conscious imitation through participation, was the decisive first step in gathering in, assimilating, knowing their way about in a musical world which had so magnetically attracted them. The Rolling Stones seemed to intuitively understand Hegel's profound insight that a going outside oneself is in a sense a return to oneself.

Clearly, this sharply developed sense of a blues tradition initially governed the musical ambit of the Stones. Except for cutting occasional, pungent, original pseudo-blues tunes of their own, such as "Tell Me," "Heart of Stone," or "Play With Fire" (the latter, one of a bevy of songs written under the pseudonym of Nanker Phelge), the Rolling Stones for the first year or so of their career were pretty much caught up in exposing their musical roots. This they did by creatively documenting the history of the blues, especially brash, hard-driving Chicago style rhythm and blues. Their 'gutsy' recordings of Chuck Berry's "Come On," Buddy Holly's "Not Fade Away," Bobby Womack's "It's All Over Now," Willy Dixon's "Little Red Rooster" – these were the exciting hits that suddenly catapulted the Stones into international prominence alongside the already myth-shrouded Beatles and near-legendary Bob Dylan.

However, "The Last Time," an original Jagger/Richard composition released in March 1965, signaled the coming of increasingly ominous musical changes for the Rolling Stones, relentless changes that were to continue almost exponentially over the following years. At the very end of this song Mick's insane, shrieking "No!, No!, No!, No!!" counterpoint to the distant, final chorus of a recurring "Maybe the last time" convincingly embodied a phantom terror bordering on the demonic. This uncanny backdrop to a looming dread was sardonically to emerge immediately afterwards in "Satisfaction," build on itself through "Get Off My Cloud" and "19th Nervous Breakdown," and erupt monstrously full-blown in early 1966 with "Paint It Black."

Although "Paint It Black" is *the* brilliant musical comet to be traced in the arc of this transitional chapter, first a few passing remarks concerning the watershed Jagger/Richard hit "Satisfaction" must be proffered here, even if it has been discussed far more rigorously in a previous chapter. For "Satisfaction" was unmistakably the pivotal work in the musical re-orientation of the Rolling Stones. It was a dramatic reversal proclaiming that from here on the Stones would strive ceaselessly to attain a shifting, yet agonizing authenticity by allowing an unflinching, solid sense of themselves to thematically dominate their finely-honed sense of a blues tradition. Consequently, more courageously than any other group, they had begun to use themselves as their own subject matter: the Rolling Stones not so much as pop stars, or possibly even rock musicians, but as genuine individuals, and rather straight-forward ones at that. As the remarkably laconic Keith Richard himself has put it:

> The music says something very basic and simple, man. Which, I don't know, exasperates. …It's all there, you've only got to look at what's in front of you. And that's all we've ever been trying to do. Not trying to tell people where to go or which way to go because I don't know. We're all following. I mean, it's all going to happen. It's all coming down.[ii]

Keeping ourselves to Keith's implied dictum of an achieved simplicity of vision, the tight-fisted lyrics of "Satisfaction" leapt out of their purely personal cosmos and landed in the total *Gestalt* of an entire generation trying to swim against the roaring current of a dehumanizing Western civilization gone completely 'mad,' that is, hyper-technological. Camus had written in his *Notebooks* that "There was a whole civilization to be re-made," and the Stones together with their generation had awakened to accept the challenge. As a result, it is not for nothing that "Satisfaction" instantly became *the* international anthem of rock music. Indeed, this song was so explosive that it was more than just mere music. It was emotional dynamite which not only shook the body, but more importantly, shouted directly to the 'soul.' Because of "Satisfaction," the Rolling Stones could no longer be conveniently dismissed as "five unfolding switchblades" – overnight they became symbols incarnate of revolution inchoate. They were now among the leaders of a generation determined to build the biggest cultural monument to itself in the history of mankind. However, to understand what the Stones are mirroring here, one does not have to unnecessarily break bones in one's head by losing oneself in the abysmal labyrinth of current Western philosophy. Fortunately, the invisible thread of Ariadne leads directly to the daily light of our glaring present and seductively beyond. The visible diffusion of the universal appeal harboring the underlying 'message' of "Satisfaction" is so widespread that flashes of it are even reflected out of a work such as *The Party* (1971), an otherwise unexceptional pornographic novel by Reneé Auden:

> Jagger was singing. He sang, and suddenly he was not frail any more, or tired. His slender body was taut with vitality and hidden power, his beautiful-ugly face, expressive as only such a face can be, ran the gamut of emotions, from sneering cynicism to intense longing – a longing for something he could not name. Felicity understood him, understood his need for excess, for pushing things to their limit. *Mick, my brother – I too can't get no satisfaction. Take me with you …I too want to be one of the damned …* (p. 47).

It would seem that for a growing number of us Spengler's *The Decline of the West* is far more than just the title of a famous book...

After "Satisfaction" the steam-rolling dread embedded within the Rolling Stones' hard-rocking lyrics furiously gathered momentum: a surrealistic, urban nightmare-world reminiscent of Fritz Lang's *Metropolis* was tensely pictured in "Get Off My Cloud," and a pitiable case of Sisyphean mental disintegration was mockingly portrayed in "19th Nervous Breakdown." All the same, if these 'smash' hits were not proof enough that the Stones had shattered the reigning lyrical orthodoxy of puerile pop music – with its insipid, clichéd cycle of love/jealousy/lament – the dread-ridden tone starting to color their darkening musical landscape became nihilistically prevalent when the Rolling Stones by-passed the blues to "Paint It Black," an instant gold-record single released in May 1966.

Eerily shot through with a haunting, profound ambivalence that somehow excites, yet disturbs, "Paint It Black" still constitutes one of the most original compositions ever produced by the Stones, or any other group in the star-studded annals of rock music for that matter. Tagged as 'raga-rock' by even the most superficial of observers and critics, this song was undeniably indicative of the astonishing musical alchemy the Rolling Stones were capable of creating when they had become full-fledged performers of their own unique material. And make no mistake about it, as a rare concocted potion of ethereal magic mixed with earthy 'funk,' this landmark work literally 'works' on the deepest subliminal recesses of the contemporary psyche. The complete emotional antipodes to the later equally brilliant, 'Yes-saying' "Jumpin' Jack Flash" (released in May 1968), "Paint It Black" is the scintillating sword of an enterprising Alexander which cruelly cuts through the enigmatic Gordian knot of twentieth-century existence to its stark terrifying core. Moreover, though there is a demonic negative quality blatantly overriding this song which cannot be ignored – a quality that was to persist through "Mother's Little Helper," "Have You Seen Your Mother, Baby, Standing In The Shadow?," and not be fully resolved until the *aere perennius*[1] album, *Their Satanic Majesties Request*, at the end of 1967 – it was an unquestionable triumph for the Rolling Stones that they were able to harness this negative outpouring and convert it so successfully into positive, if

---

[1] "More enduring than bronze": quotation from Horace's *Odes*, III, 30.1.

unsettling, musical constructs. Of course, the obvious source of this negative outflow was the biographical life-world of the Stones themselves, but exactly why this negative dimension loomed so largely at the time is a matter we shall be forced to confront in the existentially-oriented actual elucidation of "Paint It Black."

It must be recalled that although prolific songwriters Mick Jagger and Keith Richard were the prominent twin pillars giving rise to the unfolding musical arch of the Rolling Stones, Brian Jones was the vitally suspended keystone holding it majestically in place above the precarious ground of the seething *Zeitgeist*, or 'spirit of the age.' The original founder and leader of the group, the most articulate to the press, and by far always the most versatile as an instrumentalist, Brian was a major contributor of crucial importance to the Stones' music, not through writing but through sound. His remarkable abilities in this latter capacity stemmed from a rich musical background which gave him a firm foundation upon which to subsequently develop his prodigious talent. In an unauthorized biography, *Rolling Stones*, edited by David Dalton, Dalton succinctly says:

> Brian grew up in a musical family, …his mother taught piano and his father, an aircraft engineer, also

'tickled the ivories' from time to time. He was the only Stone who could read music and had studied theory as a child. When Rock began experimenting with Indian and electronic music in 1966, Brian was one of the few musicians with enough versatility to handle these developments. (p. 17)

"He was a cat who could play any musical instrument," according to Keith,[iii] and we only have to look at Brian's massive contribution to *Aftermath* (released in June 1966), the first of all future Rolling Stones' albums solely containing their own original material and featuring "Paint It Black" as the lead-off 'cut,' to see that Keith was not simply eulogizing. Coming hot on the heels of *December's Children (And Everybody's)* and *Big Hits (High Tide and Green Grass)*, *Aftermath* was for the Stones the breakthrough album defining a set of contemporary dilemmas. On it Brian played guitars, harmonicas, marimbas, bells, dulcimer, sitar, piano, organ, and harpsichord – no less than nine instruments! Indeed *Aftermath* is a typical example of what Brian actually did for the Rolling Stones: specifically, he creatively lateralized the essentially monolithic thrust of their sound, re-interpreted it by giving it delicately nuanced fullness, a measureless breadth which it would otherwise not possess. Thus, paradoxically, for many of us the Stones' music became a significant existential yard-stick by which to measure and render more coherent the invisible parameters, the opaque horizons of our own experience within the great buzzing confusion of today's world.

Therefore, if we are to ask ourselves, as we certainly must, who is primarily responsible for the extraordinary attempt to singlehandedly inaugurate a unique musical genre in "Paint It Black," to no one's surprise the answer is quite simply, Brian Jones. For by masterfully employing the exotic sound of the Indian sitar, Brian was able to lay down a ringing series of buzzing riffs which subtly incorporated a hybrid 'raga-rock' underpinning to the song's bare thematic structure. This had the effect of pervading the song with a subliminal fusion of feeling with meaning that was awesome in terms of both its magnitude and direction. This is not mere conjecture, for in a personal interview which must be regarded as a goldmine of potential philosophical insights about the Rolling Stones that are waiting to be dug up, no less an authority than Keith Richard himself has spoken about the personal factors involved in the Stones' actual recording of "Paint It Black":

> Mick wrote it. I wrote the music, he did the words. Get a single together.
>
> What's amazing about that one for me is the sitar. Also the fact that we cut it as a comedy track. Bill [Wyman,

> Stones' bassist] was playing an organ, doing a takeoff of our first manager [Giorgio Gomelsky] who started his career in show business as an organist in a cinema pit. We'd been doing it with funky rhythms and it hadn't worked and he [Brian] started playing it like this ['raga-rock'] and everybody got behind it. It's a two-beat, very strange. Brian playing the sitar makes it a whole other thing.[iv]

Something was happening here to the Rolling Stones all right, and Mr. Jones seemed to know exactly what it was.

Why was the sitar so amazing for Keith in "Paint It Black"? What was so strange to him about the way Brian played it? What was the "whole other thing" opened by its employment in the song that "everybody got behind"? And more fundamentally, what was the something which was happening here to the Rolling Stones themselves, and why did Brian seem to know exactly what it was? We have deliberately served up a volley of fruitful questions at this point to indicate that Keith's timely vignette just cited is more than simply a casual anecdote or a striking incident. It is rather a profound re-collection of an event, an e-vent in the original sense of a coming-out and brute birth of something so all-inclusive that even subsequent reflection upon its significance is gradually overpowered, speech is pulverized into babble, and babble lapses into stammering incoherence. This is as finally true for Keith as it will be for those of us who have really listened to "Paint It Black," that is to say, have heard it with more than just our ears.

Be this as it may, we must endeavor to go as far as possible in retrieving "Paint It Black" from the jealous ambiguity of silence. Indeed if we focus sharply on Brian's experience of the song, we shall possess a handy interpretive key to unlock the door of his understanding which will provide concrete access to the disclosed world of "Paint It Black." Yet before beginning, an important qualification cannot be emphasized enough, and hence must be kept constantly in mind: we will never be able to understand the world that "Paint It Black" opens up and opens out without already having been there ourselves. Why is this unavoidably so? Because there can be no disclosure of a world, any world, without a first-person commitment, dear reader. Thus our journey via Brian's perspective to the world of "Paint It Black" is a vicarious return to ourselves, to the land of our own being. We should not be alarmed by all this, for it is an inextricable existential paradox recognized by contemporary thinkers such as Heidegger, Gadamer, and Ricoeur that one can understand only what one has already experienced and yet, conversely, can experience only what one has already understood. In a real sense this existential paradox is a dynamically revolving wheel supported by individual spokes radiating from the hub of human finitude.

From Brian Jones' point of view then, what kind of world is disclosed by "Paint It Black," what mood colors that world and why does it? Why did Brian radically shift the emotional axis of the song from a comic to a tragic, even nihilistic angle? How is this re-interpreted axis related to the previously mentioned invisible philosophical one around which the Rolling Stones' musical universe churns? These are heady but necessary questions which must be asked, yet it would be best to get under way by saying what "Paint It Black" was not for Brian, before attempting to indicate what it was… It was *not* a 'catchy jingle' for a paint commercial… It was *not* a disguised marching order full of racial undertones to Black Power… And finally, it was *not* a candid remembrance of things past to when Brian was once briefly an itinerant chimneysweep in his hometown of Cheltenham…

What was it then? In order to elucidate this, "Paint It Black" must be provisionally divided into its two equally primordial components – the music and the words. Admittedly, such a procedure does interpretive violence to the total subliminal impact of the song, but nevertheless there is ample redeeming value in doing so. For Brian changed the emotional axis of "Paint It Black" only *after* he knew what it was specifically about, that is, *after* he had heard the words and the unworkable bare thematic structure. Therefore the hybrid 'raga-rock' underpinning woven by his sitar riffs is itself a creative response to the meaning intended by the words, a daring attempt to transform this vector of meaning by incarnating it in the form of a powerful musical style that is a bold new genre.

As a result, even though we have split an elucidation of "Paint It Black" into its verbal and musical components, still by first writing down the actual words or lyrics of the song, then discussing its important 'raga-rock' musical genre, and finally coming to grips with the words themselves via the necessary detour of some biographical remarks, we shall be proceeding on a way that is both analogous to Brian Jones' perspective and yet will uncover a hitherto latent understanding of the song-as-a-whole. Of course it must be realized that we will here understand "Paint It Black" differently from Brian, not only because we come after him, but more basically because he did not have the opportunity of initially hearing the song as we do, in other words, with the 'raga-rock' underpinning already built into it. For us, this underpinning is a given; for Brian and the other Rolling Stones it was an achievement, a possibility which had to be actualized by being worked out. What is really important here is that we are enabled to move about in the actually disclosed world of "Paint It Black."

These are the complete lyrics of "Paint It Black" (it cannot be suggested strongly enough that these lyrics be *read*, even *sung*, while *hearing* the song on tape or record):

I see a red door and I want it painted bla-ack
No colors anymore, I want them to turn bla-ack
I see the girls walk by,
    dressed in their summer clothes
I have to turn my head
    until my darkness goes
    (Repeat after fourth stanza)
I see a line of cars and they're all painted bla-ack
With flowers and my love both never to come ba-ack
I see people turn their heads
    and quickly look away
Like a newborn baby,
    it just happens every day

I look inside myself and see my heart is bla-ack
I see my red door I must have it painted bla-ack
Maybe then I'll fade away
    and not have to face the facts
It's not easy facing up
    when your whole world is black

No more will my green sea go turn a deeper blu-ue
I could not foresee this thing happening to you-u
If I look hard enough
      into the setting sun
My love will laugh with me
      before the morning comes
      (Repeat first stanza)

Hm-hm-hm-hm-hm-hm
      -hm-hm-hm-hm-hm-hm-m-mm…
      (Repeat three more times)
I wanna see it painted, painted black
      (Hm-hm-hm- hm-hm- hm)
      black as night, black as coal
      (-hm- hm-hm- hm- hm-hm-m-mm)
I wanna see the sun
(Hm-hm-hm- hm-hm- hm)
      blotted out from the sky
      (hm-hm -hm -hm -hm -hm-m-mm)
I wanna see it painted, painted,
      (Hm-hm-hm-hm-hm-hm)
      painted, painted black – yeah!
      (hm-hm -hm-hm hm   -hm-m-mm)
Hm-hm-hm-hm-hm-hm
      -hm-hm-hm-hm-hm-hm-m-mm…
      (Repeat three more times while fading out) …

If we are properly attuned, what is happening in this song that is also happening to ourselves, as it uncannily vibrates the very fibers of our raw existence? Everything… Very well then, what is "Paint It Black" about? Nothing… Or rather, *the* Nothing. Or still better, *No*-thing. No thing in general and everything in particular. Nothing *is* fundamentally happening in "Paint It Black." Thus, in all comic seriousness, the song is a musical much ado about nothing as the Nothing, the Nothing as No-thing, No-thing as no thing in general and everything in particular… Mick Jagger's slashing voice undulates like an emotional sine curve that winds through the sitar-spun latticework that is the heart of the song. Somewhere in the dim musical space belonging to the world *dis*-closed by "Paint It Black," a frightened chorus with shut lips hums a tragic nasal whine of impending personal breakdown. Brian Jones' sitar lays down a repetitive, slightly varying series of haunting riffs which nevertheless ground the forward thrust of the song by underpinning, yet steering its anxious, speeded-up two-beat heart throb. Somehow this oriental overlay to the pulsing music literally *dis*-orients one into the whyless swirl of daily life in the Occident. Further, this odd two-beat becomes a driving dynamo of hypertense energy pounding relentlessly onward when it is mercilessly reinforced by Bill Wyman's reverberating bass and

Charlie Watts' thudding drums. Finally, like grateful strangers, Keith Richard's clipped guitar notes hypnotically follow the first flight of Brian's buzzing sitar riffs to the newly-heard, hybrid land of 'raga-rock' …

Hence "Paint It Black" is concrete proof of the profundity of Karl Jaspers' insight that music is the most intimate of all the arts because it alone directly affects one's sense of time. Moreover, according to the axioms of musicology, music is sound organized in time and time defined by the sound that fills it. Consequently any specific piece of music projects a particular sound structure which creates its own time flow and time pattern. Brian's convincing hybridization of Indian raga with rock and roll in "Paint It Black" resulted in a newly discovered sound structure commonly known as 'raga-rock.' The time flow of this particular song is governed by a two-beat rhythm that is simply an accelerated modification of the basic four-beat rhythm of rock and roll. This doubly fast rock and roll beat has the irresistible effect of not just moving the body but convulsing it. Additionally, this "very strange" rapid two-beat in the song constitutes a deep felt rejection of a standard three-beat rhythm (actually two beats plus a rest moment) which conductor Michael Tilson Thomas has said is characteristic not only of the normal human heartbeat, but of the history of Western music since the Middle Ages as well. Thus the time flow or regulated rhythm of

"Paint It Black" signifies an intentional abandonment of the normal rest moment in a standard beat as endemic to the human heart as it has been to the historical track of Western music. Why was there such a drastic altering of rhythm here, an alteration which was simultaneously a modification of one basic beat and the rejection of another? Because, on the basis of what he had heard emanating from the song's subliminal core, Brian genuinely felt that there could be no time for any rest moments in the right rhythm for "Paint It Black." For he had listened sympathetically to the song's grim tale of a sudden and violent onslaught of lethal dread. The problem was how to rhythmically express an anxious heart throb intrinsic to the nihilistic pathos embedded within the existential predicament projected by the song. The quickly surging two-beat taken up by Brian on his sitar became a compelling rhythmic solution, acting for the other Rolling Stones as an emotional catalyst which jelled "Paint It Black" into its full musical being.

On the other hand, the temporal pattern or melody of "Paint It Black" comes from Indian raga. The melody of a song is supposed to give an imaginary up and down feeling of vertical space as the song itself moves forward horizontally in time. It was this musical space from the East, the space of raga, which Brian Jones drew upon and *re*-oriented to faithfully express a 'melodic' sense of dread that would best complement his already speeded-up rock and roll rhythm of the song. Indeed, it was precisely this unexpected combination of rock rhythm and Indian melody which resulted in 'raga-rock.' However, such a term easily degenerates into a vapid cliché if it is indiscriminately applied to any group whatsoever using a sitar as mere exotic decoration on the fringes of a song, such as the Beatles' "Norwegian Wood" from their *Rubber Soul* album of late 1965. True enough, George Harrison had begun to take up the sitar via the direct influence of Ravi Shankar, but still Harrison's sitar-work on "Norwegian Wood" serves a solely ornamental function and plays no vital part in the song's musical or verbal character. But with "Paint It Black" we shall see that the situation has diametrically changed – now the rhythm and melody are in complete harmony with the actual meaning-content of the song's lyrics. Such was due to another creative instance of the inspiring musical ingenuity of Brian Jones.

It is amazing enough that somehow in the peripatetic course of his musical peregrinations Brian too had learned how to play the sitar. Even more incredible is the fact that he knew enough about the fundamental principles of raga to apply them perfectly to the agonizing *cul-de-sac* of situational nihilism projected by "Paint It Black"'s dark ubiquity of sheer dread. For raga is the fundamental element of melody in Indian music and melody is the structural basis of that music. To fully appreciate the role of raga here, one first has to realize the place of music itself in the whole life-context of Indian culture. *Nada Brahma*, Sanskrit meaning "Sound is God," is not at all a pious exaggeration because in India musical sound and musical experience are considered to be nothing less than possible steps to the realization of the self. The highest aim of Indian music then is to reveal the essence of the universe it reflects, and raga is among the vibrant means by which this same essence can be apprehended. But raga is more than simply the melodic form *par excellence* of Indian music; it is an intensely powerful musical entity which is an exhaustive concentration on a single mood or emotion by dwelling, expanding, and elaborating upon its fleeting omnipresence. Indeed there is a Sanskrit saying to aptly illustrate this *Ranjayati iti ragah*, "That which colors the minds is a raga." Like a proverbial Lockean blank tablet, so the receptive human mind can be colored or affected by the hypnotic, intense sound of a raga as it dramatically unfolds its passionate singleness of mood. Moreover this subtle process is greatly enhanced by the pervasive existence of the *Nava Rasa*, or "nine sentiments" constituting the emotional foundation of all Indian art (*rasa* literally means "juice" or "extract"). As a result, any Indian artistic creation whatsoever is supposed to be actually dominated by one of these nine sentiments. Therefore the sitarist playing a raga must convey a particular rasa to the minds of his listeners through the music alone. Being an artistic projection of the performer's 'inner spirit,' an authentic embodiment of his deepest sensibilities, it is not surprising that the overall impact of raga music is thus more emotional than intellectual. Hence the more clearly it conforms to the expression of a single mood, emotion, or sentiment, the more overwhelming will be the total effect of a raga.

Deep in the heart of the world disclosed by "Paint It Black" lies the overwhelming mood of dreaded nothing as no thing. Thus it is not for nothing, or rather it is *because of* no thing that this song is an outstanding exemplification of *Bhayanaka*, the sixth rasa, considered to embody what is frightening or fearful. Always discovered and never invented, the raga intuitively hit upon by Brian Jones is really a melodic form or time pattern consisting of a twelve-note series of sitar riffs. This twelve-note series is elaborately carried over into Keith Richard's guitar melody, as well as into the vocal patterns of Mick Jagger and the humming choral accompaniment. At the same time, each twelve-note series of the raga-like melody itself is perfectly synchronized with the rapid two-beat rhythm, creating a total effect that can be called truly awesome. In conclusion then, that "Paint It Black" is pervasively shot through with a strange eeriness of overpowering mood is due in no small measure to its haunting musical metamorphosis which Brian himself brought about with consummate feeling and skill. His impassioned ability on the sitar to breathe the breath of life (*prana*), of rasa into the song's pure raga form (*rupa*), became the significant spark which ignited the extraordinary musical electricity generated by the other Rolling Stones into the dark and moody subliminal core of "Paint It Black."

But what about this "dark and moody subliminal core"? We have seen that "Paint It Black" is unquestionably shot through with an ineluctable mood of nihilistic dread – a dread which has the shocking effect of stripping away, of shattering the smug complacency on the thin mask of average everyday life, by ruthlessly revealing the protean face of Nothingness. What then was biographically happening here vis-à-vis the Rolling Stones themselves? Is this symbolic rendering of actual life-experience in "Paint It Black" indicative that the sinister Stones were gleefully plummeting down the left-hand path to an unbridled, total Nothingness? Surely this is what the 'public' 'thought' at the time because such a shallow opinion is easy to come by and thus demands no seriously sustained reflection. For since their shadowy beginnings on the outskirts of London in the early 1960s, the Rolling Stones have been persistently locked in an uncompromising and protracted war against 'public opinion,' that anonymous ruler which tyrannizes what passes for 'thinking' in contemporary society. Indeed, always the Stones have made it patently obvious through their iconoclastic music, life-style, and values that the 'public' in this sense is to be resolutely branded Enemy Number-One. In this regard, Brian Jones spoke for all the Rolling Stones when he once said emphatically, "We believe there can be no evolution without revolution."

This ethic of revolution was far more than merely political for the Stones, it was cultural or metapolitical, and hence more fundamentally dangerous and unsettling. It challenged openly the very philosophical presuppositions buttressing and delineating the ideally existing relationships between the personal being of the individual and the collective demands of current society-at-large. Thus, if the Beatles playfully taunted, the Rolling Stones openly threatened the 'public conscience'; consequently, it is no wonder that the British Establishment in particular hated the Stones. Typical of this 'public attitude' was a lead article by Ray Coleman in *Melody Maker*, a well-known British music paper: "Would You Let Your Sister Go With A Rolling Stone?"

Virtually everything about the Rolling Stones offended the watchful eye of the 'public,' but among the most offensive of their abrasive predilections was an increasing involvement with the drug scene around the end of 1965. To be sure both rock music and drugs constitute the rich nucleus of the emerging counterculture, and hence the Stones were no different in their propensities here than millions of their generational counterparts around the world. For example, obviously summing up the general feelings of a *whole* generation as well as the group itself, Rolling Stones' guitarist Mick Taylor (Brian Jones' successor) has remarked in a fairly recent magazine devoted to the Stones: "Because of pop music and drugs, a lot of good things have happened."[v] But both the style and theme of singles such as "Paint It Black" show that the Rolling Stones during this time were becoming deeply embedded in the drug scene in a dangerous and potentially destructive way, which other groups of the first rank such as the Beatles somehow managed to avoid. In this respect too, Brian Jones was ahead of the other Stones. According to Anita Pallenberg, Keith Richard's wife but Brian's former girlfriend, Brian was the first Rolling Stone into acid. Indeed Anita has vividly reminisced about her and Brian's initial exposure to it:

> Everybody was turning on to acid, young and beautiful and then a friend of Brian's died and it affected him very much. It made it seem as if the whole thing was a lie …The first time Brian and I took acid we thought it was like smoking a joint. We went to bed. Suddenly we looked around and

all these Hieronymus Bosch things were flashing around. That was in 1965.[vi]

What are we to make of this curious piece of testimony? …the death of Brian's close friend due to acid and his feeling that "the whole thing was a lie"? …the hallucinogenic images of seemingly irrational figures out of Bosch's rich yet puzzling panorama of profound pessimism, the triptych *The Garden of Delights*? We would do well to remember that this disturbing work's central panel about life on earth depicts the unending repetition of Knowledge as the Original Sin of Western man, and furthermore tends to celebrate what it is meant to condemn – namely, the guilty innocence of a struggling mankind doomed to be perpetual prisoner of its insatiable appetites without so much as a hint for the possibility of Salvation. Is all of this significant for an understanding of Brian's experience of "Paint It Black"? We most assuredly think so …The fact that he went so far as to radically shift the emotional axis of the song from a comic to a tragic, even nihilistic angle seems proof enough there was a meaningful fusion of experiential horizons here between Brian's total life-world and the disclosed world of "Paint It Black." This was something which the other Rolling Stones genuinely appropriated for themselves, in a basic gut-level sense, only upon Brian's intensely felt initiative.

Because he was immensely knowledgeable enough to suddenly speak about everything and anything, we have seen in previous chapters that Brian was considered to be the deep thinker of the group, deep to the point of moodiness, argumentative to the point of belligerence. However Anita Richard (née Pallenberg) has commented further that Brian's earlier experiences in the drug scene than the rest of the Stones helped create a fine existential gap between them which had not really existed hitherto.[vii] This subtle gap can be appreciated in its full significance only by now turning to and coming to grips with the actual words of "Paint It Black." For it was Brian's initial hearing of the song's lyrics which shook the foundations of his very being, which led him to decisively re-orient the concrete philosophical direction of the song.

Because of their pivotal role in the ongoing existential revolution in sensibility associated with rock music, it is no wonder that the Rolling Stones became instant catalyzing agents for massive social change. As a vital part of their all-out radical assault on the oppressive conventional values of their own culture, even the Stones' lyrics have always 'played' the unsettling function of heightening the stark realism of their hard-rocking music. In this regard "Paint It Black" stands out as a milestone work which mirrors the brutally honest, harsh world-view of the Rolling Stones with an almost unbearable emotional intensity. Just as in really seeing

Edvard Munch's *The Scream* (1895), so in really hearing "Paint It Black," we feel touched to the quick by a desperate cry mired deep in the ebony-like bowels of a dread-ful anxiety. For, like a gleaming black diamond, the deeply disturbing words of this harrowing song cut and cleave through the brittle glass armor shielding our fleeting individual selfhood. If one can initially withstand the sheer saying-power of "Paint It Black," one quickly understands that it is not we who grasp the meaning of this onrushing song, but rather its disclosive meaning which unexpectedly seizes us by our very existential roots. Without a doubt we have been violently *de-distantiated* here, as it were, from being idly curious spectators to imprisoned participants caught up in the song's projected life-world. Moreover, it is the world-disclosive power of its explosive words which originally generated, yet now brings to a stand the eery gush of its stampeding musicality, so that we may more fully experience "Paint It Black"-as-a-whole for what it truly is ...a cameo work of art whose concrete existential theme is, *à la* Kazantzakis, a terrifying 'Cretan glance' at the nothing-ing of Nothingness. An American philosopher of art, Albert Hofstadter, has written: "In art a certain absoluteness of existence is in fact arrived at by man."[viii] The fact that this "certain absoluteness of existence" comes to a stand in the primordial happening of "Paint It Black" is confirmation once again of the Rolling Stones' defiant apocalyptic ability to viscerally affect the thinking of an entire generation.

Within the uncanny purview of Mick Jagger's brilliantly written, profoundly felt lyrics of "Paint It Black" lurks an implicit awareness of Norman O. Brown's poignant reply to Herbert Marcuse: "Behind the reality of Marx lies the deeper reality of Nietzsche." Of course Marcuse immediately dismissed the existential import of this essential remark in the same disbelieving manner that Abbie Hoffman virtually did when he penned Mick "the Myra Breckinridge of the Woodstock Nation." Hoffmann, to put it mildly, had been somewhat less than pleased with Jagger's terse decline of Abbie's previous request for money to aid his fellow 'Chicago Seven' at their notorious political trial in late 1969 – "We've got trials of our own," Mick had abruptly quipped at the time. But Abbie not merely *mis*-understood what Mick had meant here, he had understandably *un*-understood him. For Jagger in effect had subtly hinted that the Rolling Stones were incessantly undergoing trials which were far closer to Kafka than to a Chicago courtroom; if we are careful to not so much cross-examine but really listen to the disconcerting lyrics of songs such as "Paint It Black," we too shall hear the inescapable authentic truth of Mick's timely self-observation overwhelmingly present in this carefully wrought Jagger/Richard composition.

"We'll make them eat their lousy words one day. We'll make them take our music seriously,"[ix] Brian Jones had once angrily commented about the typically mindless remarks of journalists who simply inflamed the dark light of the 'public' that constantly obscures everything truly significant concerning the Rolling Stones. Indeed, even a cursory reading of Mick's weighty lyrics of "Paint It Black" demands that we keep Brian's prophetic contention close to heart, as we try to understand with our guts instead of merely with our heads the fundamental existential vector of meaning drawing the song in its primordial wake. Therefore, in order to considerably deepen the elucidation of its verbal dimension, "Paint It Black"'s thought-provoking lyrics must now be tentatively divided into two appropriate horizons of overlapping existential relevance – the psychological and the ontological. We shall eventually see that the afore-mentioned fine existential gap between Brian and the other Stones was itself founded upon and grew out of Jones' explicit as opposed to Jagger's implicit awareness of this all-encompassing ontological horizon suddenly disclosed by the awesome saying-power of the song.

Within the biographical ambit of the psychological, the horizon most apparently related directly to the actual life-world of the Rolling Stones themselves, particularly Mick's own life-situation, we encounter a vivid symbolic description of the anguished onslaught of suicidal depression-about-to-become-mental collapse. At this personal level the words of "Paint It Black" disclose what Jaspers would call a 'limit-situation,' an archetypal situation happening within an individual's life-world so extreme in its existential tension that its experiential outer boundaries or limits are those of the human condition-as-such, and thus cannot be changed or surmounted, only acknowledged. "I must die, I must suffer, I must struggle, I am subject to chance, I involve myself inexorably in guilt,"[x] Jaspers dramatically philosophizes: these limit-situations, however fraught with dread, are the inescapable realities in relation to which alone human existence can be made genuinely meaningful. A tabooed topic as a *normal* social experience, elementary reflection confirms that mental collapse, mental illness is not an exceptional breakdown, but a prevalent condition, a typical limit-situation, part of the ordinary routine of everyday living in advanced technological society. Consequently the intensive psychic disintegration co-extensive with the projected life-world of "Paint It Black" must be regarded as a permanent structural feature of our whole way of life, of our civilization, and not simply the random psychological stance of a despairing individual.

Despite the oppressive social matrix of cultural atomization that remains the general truth about the personal reality of existential 'shipwreck,' still we are utterly shocked by the sheer emotional intensity of "Paint It Black"'s nihilistic pathos. But like the pitiless reflection in a mirror gazing back at ourselves, we are gripped here by the shock of self-recognition, a stern recognition of the fact that we all must pay an exorbitant psychic cost for living the time of waiting for the 'not yet.' The old gods no longer exist, the new ones have not yet appeared, and a grinding pessimism desperately bemoans the unlikelihood of the latter. "One must be an individualist, otherwise one remains a mass-man," Jagger once casually aphorized in a German press interview, but "Paint It Black" clearly reveals authentic individuality to be an agonizing achievement, as difficult only as it is rare, which can very well mean an unanticipated, abrupt crossing-over into the disrupting underworld of a full-blown madness. Ironically, the song shows that darkness can be fatally enlightening in the asymptotic personal encounter with the paralyzing Janus-face of Nothingness. This is what makes "Paint It Black" such a waking nightmare (a daymare?), a ballooning darkness at noon for a manic mind at the end of its existential tether. We are pulled apart by a deep seated ambivalence that rivets yet terrifies as the song's lyrics relentlessly delineate its protagonist's aporetic limit-situation in poetic stanzas stressing in high relief its intimate psychological complementarity of color and mood.

No doubt about it, a dark and demanding quotidian mood blackly colors the threatening world of "Paint It Black." It is dark because this anguished mood is a frightful dread so black it is colorless – "No colors anymore I want them to turn bla-ack…" (first stanza). It is demanding because this frenzied mood doesn't just passively color the protagonist's life-world, it passionately paints it the colorlessly blackest of all possible blacks, since the protagonist has looked inside himself and sees that his heart too is already black (third stanza). Everything is to be blindly painted this ultimate non-color: the protagonist's red door, all colors, a line of cars, his former beloved. This raving nihilistic fervor is supremely consummated by a demand to have the very sun itself "blotted out from the sky" (last stanza). Finally, it is quotidian because this persistent mood as helplessly comes – "I see people turn their heads / and quickly look away / Like a newborn baby / it just happens every day…" (second stanza) – as it mysteriously vanishes – "I see the girls walk by / dressed in their summer clothes / I have to turn my head / until my darkness goes…" (first stanza). To be sure, there is a fleeting feeling of lost reminiscence laced with a trace of laughter about midway through the song – "No more will my green sea go turn a deeper blue…" etc. (whole fourth stanza) – but this has already been obliterated by a willful urge to self-destruction, to "fade away," because of a staunch personal refusal to face the nagging resistance of naked reality, since "It's not easy facing up / when your whole world is black…" (third stanza). We ourselves feel tightly caught in the lethal grip of Freud's *Thanatos*, or 'Death instinct.'

Unquestionably gone from "Paint It Black" is the saving grace of the self-mocking, comic braggadocio underlying "Satisfaction"; indeed, so serious is the basic existential thrust of the former that the latter seems almost routine, even vaudeville by comparison. As a result, we should not be overly surprised that Brian Jones initially took much closer to heart the overall philosophical meaning of "Paint It Black" than did the other Rolling Stones, Mick Jagger included. Brian's omnivorous mind, his enormously sensitive intelligence, and his earlier involvement in the drug scene have already been cited as key factors in the inexorable germination of his personal existential gap vis-à-vis the other Stones. This would go far in explaining Jones' somewhat natural affinity for the nihilistic psychodrama being played out in the harrowing verbal arena of "Paint It Black," but is it adequate? Hardly. In the further exploratory course of *Unrolled Stone*, we propose to show conclusively that Brian Jones' not atypical emotional constitution was simply not stable enough to existentially assimilate the sheer intellectual weight of his own expanding philosophical awareness gnawing painfully at his vitals. Our working hypothesis is not mere wishful supposition. Looking ahead to the Rolling Stones' notorious 1967 drug busts and trials, *Rolling Stone* magazine carried a brief news item of vital importance concerning Brian's then current emotional state, an excerpt from which must now be quoted:

> …The sentence was handed down despite a psychiatrist's evidence that Jones' mental health would be completely destroyed by confinement. 'He would go into psychotic depression as he could not possibly stand a stigma of a prison sentence, and he might well attempt to injure himself,' argued Dr. Leonard Henry, who treated Jones for a breakdown after his arrest last May…
> (Nov. 23, 1967, p. 4).

Lest anyone be so eager here to cast the first stone, it would be wise to remember a pithy maxim by Nietzsche: "Even the most courageous among us only rarely has the courage for that which he really knows."[xi] It is precisely this existential predicament which is the real gut-level issue at stake in this book, for we suspect that what was true here for Brian Jones is in essence equally valid for the Rolling Stones themselves, together with the whole generation for whom they are acknowledged spokesmen *par excellence*. This is the crucial experiential source originally accounting for the overlapping existential relevance of the psychological and ontological horizons characteristic of "Paint It Black"'s eery lyrics. As Brian himself later wrote with such haunting clairvoyance in his liner-notes to *Joujouka*, a uniquely brilliant album which he recorded and produced with considerable expertise of the traditional Moroccan music played at the Rites of Pan Festival, and which was posthumously released in October 1971 – "Such psychic weaklings has Western civilization made of so many of us…"

Within the already indicated philosophical ambit of the ontological, the all-encompassing horizon of horizons that is really nearest to us in spite of its apparent farness, we at last reach the total *Gestalt* of "Paint It Black" itself, because in ontology we have finally attained the most fundamental and hence all-embracing perspective within the philosophical enterprise *per se* dealing with the basic features and structures of existence, that *is to say*, "Being" …At this universal level intimately grounding "Paint It Black," the existential breakdown typical of the psychological horizon becomes an awesome breaking-open, a breaking-out, a breakthrough into the icy region of meaning shoring up the brutally honest, harsh world-view of the Rolling Stones themselves. If one's ears are carefully attuned, this same song shrilly trumpets what R.

D. Laing has called *the* 'ontological insecurity' uncannily lurking at the very bottom of our godless time. Is it any wonder that their countless 'fans' still in-sanely shriek "We want the Stones!"? The common wave-length of mutual feeling and tacit understanding effortlessly linking the Rolling Stones to their own generation actually transmits a shared ontological message whose grim underside is savagely reflected in "Paint It Black"'s dread-ful lyrics. We must now let ourselves be captured by, yet reflect upon its dark reflection, if we are to genuinely come to grips with and interpretively unroll the creeping ontological message of the song's nihilistic, 'No-saying power' …'Such psychic weaklings has Western civilization made of so many of us…' Why is this? …

As a profound artistic statement which ontologically 'works' as a primary happening of truth in the vast primordial field of our potentially authentic being, "Paint It Black" is a passionate answer to the genuine questioning that originally places in the open the question about the very meaning of contemporary existence. Thus, we have just re-stood this question in its proper ontological place in the timely hope that "Paint It Black"'s answer can be more fully understood as an answer. And what is the song's all-inclusive answer? Simply that the solution to the question about the very meaning of contemporary existence is seen to be not in the dissolution of the question, *à la* Wittgenstein or Zen, but in the dissolution of the questioner himself, the one who truthfully dares to ask the presumably answerless question in the first place, *à la* nihilism. "Paint It Black"'s gut-wrenching lyrics have violently overturned the classic Socratic maxim of "Know thyself" and replaced it with the self-destructing ethos of a universal indictment whose verdict is "Guilty as charged!" and whose sentence spares Nothing in a chaotic Kirillovian ukase of cosmic-coupled with self-annihilation – "I want to see the sun / blotted out from the sky…" (last stanza). "I have searched myself and found nothing!," the song's hysterical protagonist in effect tragically announces through his crazed body in frenzied nihilistic acts of vicariously smearing everything, including existence itself, "black as night, black as coal…" (last stanza). The adjudged absolute meaninglessness of contemporary existence expressed here has ruthlessly come home to roost in that null-point of non-meaning, the protagonist's own person-less 'being' – "Maybe then I'll fade away / and not have to face the facts / It's not easy facing up – when your whole world is black…" (third stanza). We have already declared that "Paint It Black" reveals that Nothingness reveals itself by Nothing-ing, in short, as Bob Dylan sardonically sings – "Nothing *is* revealed…". However, the Rolling Stones' later 'Yes-saying,' "Jumpin' Jack Flash"-like delirious celebration of this basic ontological truth is completely beyond the emotional pale of "Paint It Black"'s utterly terrified protagonist. He cannot withstand standing face to the Janus-face of ambivalent Nothingness as it uncannily nothings, and so he goes under rather than understand that one cannot demand answers from existence – one can only let oneself be questioningly called by, yet through existence itself. Those who can hear will be able to answer to this silent call from *No*-thing by co-responding. Hence to revile Nothing-as-revealed is to blindly re-veil it in the black mist of nihilism. Nevertheless, the dark ontological arrow that is "Paint It Black" paradoxically points out to us that one is perhaps never closer to one's own existential roots than while undergoing the rampaging hammer-blows of emotional disintegration. This is remarkably congruent with Laing's laconic notion in *The Politics of Experience* that madness as break-down "may also be breakthrough" (p. 133). In any case, the protagonist's personal identity in "Paint It Black" is not allowed to passively fly out the gaping window of self-awareness, it simply suffers 'shipwreck' on the triumphant shoals of mortal *life*. Judging from the total *Gestalt* of this radically disturbing song, the Rolling Stones themselves may well be rich psychiatric 'raw material,' but they have also incidentally irrefutably changed from the ground up the cultural topography of today's world… "Such psychic weaklings has Western civilization made of so many of us…" How so 'so many'?…

In essence, the overall philosophical upshot of "Paint It Black" is that its barely hidden ontological leitmotiv can be drawn from the deep, inexhaustible well of Heidegger's thought; the abysmal experience that "Dread reveals Nothing" potentially avails our primordial understanding of existence as Being because only this same limit-ing experience can un-veil the shuddering *in*-sight that "Man is the place-holder of Nothing-ness," itself the "veil of Being." We, however, tend to ontologically experience this precarious icy region of dis-closive meaning *pro*-jected by "Paint It Black" as a raging ocean of rampant universal meaninglessness in which our culturally atomized personal being itself dissolves, as it were, because so many of us have already been made psychic weaklings by Western civilization, according to Brian Jones' self-penetrating cultural glance. It would seem Brian ironically possessed the uncanny existential strength to draw the other Rolling Stones into the ambivalent ontological perspective of his own visceral awareness by letting them explicitly real-ize, in the irrupting nihilistic pathos uncontrollably welling up from the very guts of this haunting song, that here was not merely a harmless piece of hard-charging musical claptrap, but that here too the 'Dreadful has already happened,'[xii] that what is termed 'metaphysical anxiety' in the sanitized argot of current academic philosophy has become the 'normal' twentieth century condition of ontological insecurity typifying a technologically disoriented, literally planet-ary humanity. Therefore, an implicit, yet decisive consequence of its ontological 'spin-off' effect is that "Paint It Black" constitutes from a strictly cultural standpoint a desperate and terrifying Parthian shot angrily aimed directly at the subsisting ossified core of our entire contemporary Western existence. For the song's agonized protagonist virtually asks the all-important, terrible question that he cannot answer affirmatively – "Shut up within the expanding one-dimensional iron cage that is contemporary Western civilization, how can I say 'Yes!' to Life?" Is not the tentacular planetary spread of this same civilization essentially an external symptom, a reflection of its own internal *dis*-ease, the fatal disease that is strikingly incarnated in the vivid nihilistic vortex of "Paint It Black"? Not only has the sun of existential certainty also set on the troubled waters of the protagonist's dread-ful being, but are not we ourselves, in a blinding flash of chilling truthfulness, shaken to our very ontological foundations by the sudden subliminal suspicion escaping like a black gas from the song that the twentieth century has been the historical assassin of overarching significance, that the blazing corona of all-embracing meaning ringing our cultural *raison d'être* has somehow gone out? Thus, it is through the body, what Merleau-Ponty has called 'the lived-body,' in its concrete capacity as the ultimate locus of existential meaning that "Paint It

Black" as music communicates the cogent quotation dis-covered by Nietzsche regarding the shattered cultural aftermath of this supreme historical happening: 'Nothing is true, everything is permitted.'[xiii] This emotionally ambiguous apotheosis of existential possibility not only paralyzes the song's protagonist to the point of an angry vulnerability via its *sotto voce* corollary – 'All is in vain' –, but it equally cuts down to the very marrow of our daily existence by ruthlessly exposing its deceptively spangled superfluity. Moreover, we shall see in a later chapter of *Unrolled Stone* that this cryptic quotation cited by Nietzsche will return again to plague us when it is casually reiterated by Mick Jagger's spiritual Siamese-twin, Turner, in Mick's out-standing film *Performance*… 'Nothing is true, everything is permitted' – 'All is in vain.' Was this not the same grinding intellectual weight, the billowing philosophical awareness gnawing painfully at Brian Jones' vitals? And what does this bound Prometheus of the Rolling Stones fate-fully utter here on his own behalf? … 'Such psychic weaklings has Western civilization made of so many of us…'

In our attempted philosophization of the Rolling Stones as all-encompassing historical ciphers, *à la* Jaspers, to be existentially de-ciphered, *à la* Heidegger, we must beware of lapsing into the half-baked sociologizing of the mass-media that is prone to mindlessly sensationalize the vital significance of the Stones by conveniently pigeonholing them in some comfortable 'jive-ass' niche such as the 'Social Discontent of Youth' or the 'Youth Culture.' Like the current abortive efforts in Anglo-American academic philosophy, such myopic evaluations remain permanently blinded by an insulting 'clarity' as well as a not-so-profound 'knowledge' of the obvious. On the contrary, we have tried to show in the case of "Paint It Black" that it is precisely because of its nihilistic 'No-saying' power that this cameo work of art reflects the grim underside of a shared, concrete ontological message effortlessly linking the Rolling Stones themselves to the *Gestalt* of an entire generation. Further, we have already said that it is this icy ontological region of dreadful meaning which shores up the brutally honest, harsh world-view of the Stones. Without a doubt, this is a coherent world-view whose antipodal emotional extremes are peripherally embodied with almost unbelievable force in their *non plus ultra* music, on the one hand by the *life-denying* "Paint It Black," and on the other by the later *life-affirming* "Jumpin' Jack Flash." But what about the structural features of this pervasive world-view? What are some of its dominant elements that are ontologically shored up and inchoately brought to a stand in an archetypal song such as "Paint It Black"? We shall have to wait until the concluding chapters of *Unrolled Stone* to rigorously undertake a proper thoughtfully-oriented, existential elucidation of this same ramified world-view in the total context of the Rolling Stones' actual lives, together with the whole body of their music, but its unquestionably *Demian*-like aura can be sketched here simply in its bare skeletal form.

Like Hesse's Max Demian, the Rolling Stones are the legitimate offspring of Nietzsche, mythic 'December's Children' suddenly become 'Everybody's' in the dark and agonizing winter of our crisis-riddled, all but 'broken' historical epoch. Lest it be thought that we exaggerate here, in what would be an excellent commentary on the already-discussed, several philosophical motifs underpinning the total *Gestalt* of "Paint It Black," Nietzsche himself has prophetically uttered with a still-contemporary ring of eery profundity:

> My friends, it was hard for us when we were young: we suffered youth itself like a serious sickness. That is due to the time into which we have been *thrown* – a time of extensive inner decay and disintegration, a time that with all its weaknesses, and even with its best strength, opposes the spirit of youth. Disintegration characterizes this time, and thus uncertainty: nothing stands firmly on its feet or on a hard faith in itself; one lives for tomorrow, as the day after tomorrow is dubious. Everything on our

way is slippery and dangerous, and the ice that still supports us has become thin: all of us feel the warm, uncanny breath of the thawing wind: where we still walk, soon no one will be able to walk.[xiv]

This timely section from Nietzsche's *The Will to Power*, the nihilistic chaos of a dread-ful existential limit-situation nakedly disclosed in the musical time-space of "Paint It Black," and the brutally honest, harsh world-view of the Stones themselves, tacitly fused with the invisible quasi-metaphysical yearnings of a whole generation – all reverberate with the same essential historical givens constitutive of present day existence: (1) the utter ontological fluidification, the thoroughgoing philosophical fragmentation of all reality, especially with regard to the basic existential features and structures of human being; (2) a concomitant nagging sense of existential homelessness that has unmistakably become something like a shared world destiny… Even though *Unrolled Stone* is only directly concerned with the Rolling Stones here, to extensively comment now on this skeletal interpretive scheme would be singularly unwise, like picking potentially choice fruit prematurely – rather this as yet undeveloped scheme must be allowed to steadily ripen in subsequent chapters within the comprehensive context of the Stones' historical evolution, before being thoroughly elucidated in the final part of this exploratory book by means of the grasping power of by then more concretely-rooted and fully-developed concepts. What is finally gathered in as the sustained harvest of thought, first must be modestly seeded in the furrowed fields of the heart.

In conclusion, as the lead-off 'cut' on *Aftermath* and the later *Through the Past, Darkly* (*Big Hits Vol. 2*), "Paint It Black" deservedly remains among the greatest of a growing cluster of great Rolling Stones' hits arising in the aftermath of their authentic destruction of conventional pop music. In fact, since then, we shall soon show in upcoming chapters that the Stones have become something of a major influence on the musical traditions which first influenced them. Still, we have tried to indicate in this chapter that we shall not be able to wholly understand the Rolling Stones themselves in their vital capacity as *the* soundtrack of modern times, as living myths miraculously existing in a technological age gone crystalline in its mythlessness, without already having come to grips with and understood the shadowy track of Brian Jones' enigmatic life. For, make no mistake about it, like a tightly-fitted triad of successively contained boxes constituting an intricate Chinese puzzle, the Rolling Stones are the historically significant riddle-to-be-deciphered that is cloaked within the enigma-to-be-unrolled of Brian's haunting existence, which itself is wrapped within the abiding mystery of *the* question-to-be-interrogated concerning the very meaning of our current historical epoch. Indeed, in this regard we would do well to heed closely Brian Jones' own poetic premonition inscribed on the inside cover of the curiously Stop-sign shaped *Through The Past, Darkly*, a memorial album posthumously released in his honor in September 1969, a scant two months after his untimely death at the bottom of his Cotchford Farm swimming pool:

> When this you see, remember me
> and bear me in your mind
> Let all the world say what they may,
> speak of me as you find

As Charles Reich has magnificently rhapsodized about their music in *The Greening of America*:

> Not even the turbulent fury of Beethoven's Ninth Symphony can compete for sheer energy with the Rolling Stones (p. 266)

Hopefully we too have captured in this chapter about "Paint It Black" some of the 'spirit' and the magic of the Rolling Stones. Perhaps we immediately identify with them in the deepest subliminal recesses of our being, because in a very real sense we seem to instinctively know with an unflagging conviction that like it or not, existentially we are all Rolling Stones…[xv]

L.T. Stallings

Westhampton Beach, Long Island
November 18, 1972

Brian's Personal Space Odyssey –
"2000 Light Years From Home"
RIP

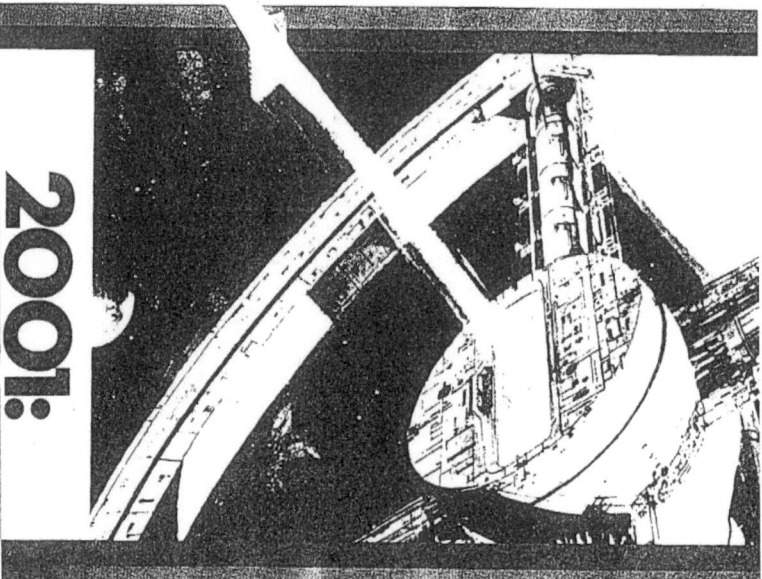

Endnotes

[i] Because of this heuristic simile of the Rolling Stones as a five-fingered hand, it would be appropriate at this point to state our thesis: If Mick Jagger as lead singer is the visible incarnation of the Stones' music, the *thumb* of that hand, then guitarist-instrumentalist Brian Jones was its index finger, the invisible arrow of their music aimed at the unknown. Hence the hand that is the Rolling Stones as it were not only had a firm grasp of the present, but also pointed toward the veiled horizon of the oncoming future. It is in this metaphorical sense that the hand of the Rolling Stones bears a mark of the question of a generation's destiny.

[ii] Robert Greenfield, "The Rolling Stone Interview: Keith Richard," *Rolling Stone* (August 19, 1971), p. 36.

[iii] Ibid, p. 33.

[iv] Ibid.

[v] The Rolling Stones, by the Editors of Dell, 1970, p. 17.

[vi] Robert Greenfield, op. cit., p. 30.

[vii] Ibid.

[viii] Albert Hofstadter, "Validity versus Value," *The Journal of Philosophy* (#59: October 11, 1962), p. 606.

[ix] "Brian Jones: Sympathy for the Devil," *Rolling Stone*. August 9, 1969, p. 8.

[x] Karl Jaspers, *Way to Wisdom* (translated by R. Manheim), 1951, p. 20.

[xi] Friedrich Nietzsche, *Twilight of the Idols* (translated by W. Kaufmann), "Maxims and Arrows" - #2. In: Walter Kaufmann's *The Portable Nietzsche*, 1954, p. 466.

[xii] R. D. Laing, *The Politics of Experience,* 1967, p. 54. (actually Heidegger's phrase)

[xiii] Friedrich Nietzsche, *On the Genealogy of Morals (*translated by W. Kaufmann), 1967, p. 150.

[xiv] Friedrich Nietzsche, *The Will To Power* (translated by W. Kaufmann), 1967, p. 40.

[xv] A note for the new 'philosophizers' – merely academic philosophers beware! – : this chapter is the new found land of a concrete hermeneutic praxis oriented around the ontological axis of contemporary German philosophizing, especially Heidegger's "Being-centered" thinking (*Seinsdenken*). The latter's magnum opus, *Being and Time* (*Sein und Zeit*, 1927) should be regarded as the tacit philosophical point of departure guiding the exploratory thrust of *Unrolled Stone*.

From the Doors – *Other Voices* (1971)

TIGHTROPE RIDE
(Manzarek, Krieger)

You're on a tightrope ride
Nobody by your side
Well, you're all alone
Gotta find a new home
But don't go over the line
You better keep on time
Or you'll lose your mind
On your tightrope ride.

Watch out, don't fall!   [spoken]
Careful, don't slip!

You better get your balance
You have to feel the way
There are no more questions
No answers today
There are no reasons
There are no more rhymes
But if you feel it
You can fly next time
You can fly next time
Or maybe this time.

Did you think we were all together?
Did you think we were all the same?
Did you think maybe I could help you
Remember your name
Remember the game
What's the name of the game
It's a very good game
Never stays the same
It's the number one
From the mud to the sun.

You're on a tightrope ride
We're all by your side
But you're all alone
And we're going home
And we're by your side
But you're all alone
Like a rolling stone
Like Brian Jones
On a tightrope ride
Yeah
On a tightrope ride.
On a tightrope ride
Yeah
On a tightrope ride.

Playboy, December 1972

Annex

Part A – Academia…101

Part B – Miscellaneous…110

Part C – Full Circle…119

Annex: Part A – Academia

Lecture: Sociology 1 – Basic Concepts in Sociology...102

Notes: *Hans-George Gadamer's Hermeneutic as a Critique of Historical Reason* by David Eugene Gibson...107

For Professor Sweeney (currently covering the STRUCTURE of ORGANIZATIONS)

Conklin Bldg. #5, 9:00 a.m., Friday, Dec. 10th, 1971

"From the first not a thing is" (*Platform Sutra of Hui-neng*, Chinese Chan Buddhist Patriarch, 639-713 A.D.)

Sociology 1 – Basic Concepts of Sociology

** Lecture – the CRISIS in the sociological concepts and foundations of contemporary society.

1) **Introduction** – Ladies and gentlemen, good morning, or rather being a citizen of the state of Hawaii, perhaps it would be better to say ALOHA. (Welcome to the breakfast show.) I and my associate, Miss Audrey Dykas (who incidentally is a recent graduate of this institution), have come from very far away (Honolulu), because we are en-route to England in order to write a definitive philosophical interpretation of the ROLLING STONES, which will not merely be just another book, but a carefully assembled TIME-BOMB designed to EXPLODE inside each one of your heads… However, what I have been asked by Prof. Sweeney to speak to you about today is of a slightly different nature, or "cup of tea," as it were. The remarks that I am going to share with you here do not really constitute what could be called a lecture, but rather should better be designated as a SKETCH, because of their rambling and admittedly incomplete direction.

2) **Sketch** –
   a. Philosophically (in terms of a sustained reflection upon its own unavoidably shifting foundations) sociology itself is a REGIONAL ONTOLOGY (ONTOLOGY – the study of the whole of what is) designed to illuminate the SOCIAL nature of human existence (SOCIOS in Greek means 'COMRADE,' thus implying the SHARED LIFEWORLD of the POLIS, one that was shattered in thought by the Platonic thrust of Augustine Christianity with its separate realms of the City of God and the City of Man, the Sacred and the Profane, as it were). The way this is done is by the effective GRASPING power of sociological CONCEPTS (indeed CONCIPERE literally means to 'TAKE HOLD OF' or 'GRASP' in Latin). This already mentioned social nature of human existence itself is basically structured as follows: ROLES, RULES, and INSTITUTIONS that are ultimately supported and legitimated by VALUES (BELIEFS). In other words, RRI ultimately derive FROM VALUES, and values themselves are EVALUATIONS of the totality or whole of existence in terms of its MEANING (GOOD / EVIL) by a particular society or culture (a PEOPLE)...* Read from Nietzsche's *Zarathustra* (p. 58, "on the Thousand and One Goals")... But once again returning to the way by which sociological concepts GRASP social reality, I must point out that today in the U.S. the social sciences as a whole are suffering from a massive inferiority complex, because they are desperately trying to emulate the rigor and precise results of the natural sciences. However, this shows an appalling ignorance that was

already dispelled by the really great German historian W. Dilthey at the beginning of this century when he clearly demarcated the fundamental differences between the *Naturwissenschaften* and the *Geisteswissenschaften* (the study of OBJECTS vs. SUBJECTS, or EXPLANATION vs. UNDERSTANDING).

b. Historically, of course, the beginning of sociology as a systematic discipline (A. Comte) coincides with the beginnings of the INDUSTRIAL REVOLUTION and the tremendous consequences following in its wake (URBANIZATION, the solidification of thoroughly secularized, dominant POLITICAL IDEOLOGIES, and the awesome presence of TECHNOLOGY). No one in his right mind today could possibly deny that TECHNOLOGY is the formative and shaping power on the planet (in this sense the "Europeanization" of the earth is almost complete – to say the least this secular "blessing" is a dubious one in terms of its levelling-down effect on other non-technological cultures). This means that sociology as a discipline has always been intimately wedded to the whole process of INDUSTRIALIZATION, and indeed has sought to understand the increasing fragmentation of social reality (euphemically called the "division of labor" or "specialization of roles and functions") that has been relentlessly occurring, at least in the West, since the period just after the French Revolution. Sociology thus historically has been tied up with the expansion and ever growing complexities of the city (CIVIS means

'city' in Latin, but the word is also almost synonymous with CIVILIZATION).
c. CRISIS as the CONVERGENCE of the PHILOSOPHICAL and the HISTORICAL. CRISIS in the fundamental Greek meaning of the term means a 'BREAK.' WHAT has been 'broken'? (Ask yourself that same question as you helplessly fondle your French fries in the local drive-in on a Friday night, and wonder what to do or what's happening in order to avoid the silent terror of BOREDOM!) TIME, TRADITION, HISTORY, MAN'S SELF-UNDERSTANDING, REALITY. Regarding our former comments on the crucial relation between RRI and VALUES, what if this totality is broken, shattered, how does one evaluate and from whence do RRI derive their justification and legitimacy when existing values have become bankrupt? And if ontology is fragmented how does sociology itself, or any other systematic discipline for that matter legitimate itself? Dizzying questions these are, but I have not come here to put the "fear of God" in you, so to speak, so much as the "fear of the ABSENCE of God," the DEATH of God, as the horrendous historical fact bears upon sociology as a discipline and yourselves as existentially concerned human beings in an increasingly chaotic and lopsided world.* Now read Corman's letter (5 minutes). CRISIS ~ CULTURE SHOCK (Peace Corps →conflict of WORLD-VIEWS or *Weltanschauungen* – it is not something that one has that can be easily disposed of, e.g., a suit of clothes, it is rather something that one IS – to change it one must literally think against oneself).

HISTORICISM, the RELATIVITY of VALUES, CULTURAL RELATIVITY.

Peace Corps Vignettes:
1. *Waktu adalah uang*
   (Indonesian language "time is money")
2. Hunger – stomach and watch
3. Soldiers holding hands, men and women forbidden
4. Left-hand taboo, the ritual of rectal ablutions after defecation. The CRISIS in sociology (and indeed in all intellectual endeavor, from physics → poetry) is actually a crisis in MAN-AS-SUCH. Sartre – "Nothingness lies like a worm coiled up in the heart of Being." **The problem – no one alive today knows the way out this historically unprecedented "dead end" or cul-de-sac into which Western man has almost completely "boxed" himself in. *Final reading from Nietzsche's Zarathustra (p. 60)… **Remember, don't let college get in the way of your education (it didn't for Hermann Hesse)!!

FINIS

Hans-Georg Gadamer's Hermeneutic as a Critique of Historical Reason

(David Eugene Gibson, Rice U PhD, 1968)

"…although the question of the meaning of Being is the 'most universal and the emptiest of questions' (Suz, p. 39), the question may be individualized for a particular *Dasein*. A particular *Dasein* is needed in order to have a concrete starting point for the analyses" (p. 59).

"…the average, vague understanding of Being already exists, since Dasein already has some understanding of its own Being" (p. 70).

'This guiding activity of taking a look at Being arises from the average understanding of Being in which we always operate and which in the end belongs to the essential constitution of Dasein itself.' (p. 70) (Suz, p. 39)

"When Heidegger uses the phrase 'meaning of Being,' he is pointing out the structures of some particular Dasein which make possible any understanding of Being. Hence, the question about the meaning of Being is a question about the structure of some Dasein's world, and a question about understanding is asking about that Dasein's ability to operate within these relationships. To say that Dasein 'knows his way about' is to indicate that he has sufficiently ordered his world so that he is aware of its possibilities." (p. 73)

"…the hermeneutic problem is that problem of reaching agreement about the structures of a possible world." (p. 122)

Horizontverschmelzung – "a fusion of horizons."

"Being was explicated as the relationships in the shared-world. A problem immediately arose, however, for there was no concrete objectification of these relationships; hence, for the moment, Heidegger was forced to talk of the *meaning of Being* which, in fact, was a 'view of Being.' Because a concrete objectification could only be found in a single *Dasein*, there was no direct way to approach the problem of Being. The three-fold distinction in questioning was necessary, for although the problem was still Being, the question had to be addressed to a particular *Dasein* (*das Befragte*, 'the entity which is asked *re* the question about Being') in order to discover his understanding of Being. This understanding was equivalent to the meaning of Being, or Being for a particular *Dasein*. This takes into account the statement: 'The question of the meaning of Being is the most universal and the emptiest of all questions, but at the same time it is possible to individualize it very precisely for any particular Dasein' " (Suz, p. 39) (p. 161).

{ Being – "structures of a shared-world"

Understanding – "knowing one's way about in a shared-world"

"…the meaning of Being …corresponds to an individual's understanding; hence, questioning of an individual may not accurately reflect the structures of the world" (p. 168).

*Understanding of a world = horizon (Gadamer).

"Therefore, against Heidegger, Gadamer maintains the following points.

1) …although the concept Being-in-the-world is crucial to the formulation of the concept, historical situation, the most important element of the historical situation is the agreement

about a world. Heidegger, although he recognized this feature in *Sein und Zeit*, failed to make it the center of the study...
2) ...Gadamer attempts a systematic presentation of language as the medium of experience. Of course, this study of language and its relationship to experience is guided by the explication of the concept, shared-world.
3) ...Gadamer argues that Heidegger's puns are not even in agreement with the theory of understanding which may be derived from his writings" (pp. 198-199).
4) Results established by Gadamer's writings on the hermeneutic problem:
    1. "...all understanding is based on fore-structures which must be seen in their relationship to a world shared with other persons.
    2. ...it is impossible to understand as the author did (re the instance of understanding which takes place in connection with a text from a different historical situation)...
    3. ...Gadamer answers the question about the objectification of mind by claiming that language is such an objectification that can be studied (Gadamer looks at language as the reification of the understanding)... (Language ~ objective mind)..." (pp. 199-200)

Annex: Part B – Miscellaneous

Contextuality of *Paint It Black*…111

Rolling Stones' Trademark – An Excursus…115

The Question of Joujouka…117

Contextuality of *Paint It Black*

(A riveting, terrifying *limit situation*)

1. PIB re *Aftermath.*
2. PIB re Brian Jones' life.
    a. *Through the Past, Darkly.*
    b. *Joujouka* (PIB message – don't mind losing your mind once in a while – it's normal).

Freedom as freedom for *meaning* and a freeing from *nihilism*. Rolling Stones as existential revolutionaries – a defiant apocalyptic warning of what the future has in store for us (a visceral anarchism).

Theme – the disruption of average everydayness by ANXIETY (it UNHINGES complacency).

PIB a waking nightmare – a daymare!

DIS-orienting quality of the song.

Darkness can be enlightening.

(*Individuelles Dasein*) Throws one BACK on oneself.

The revolution is personal (sex and drugs) (a-political, yet bold new attitudes involved).

* "Nothing is true, everything is permitted." (all is in vain)

Life as performance, willingness to experiment with a variety of unconventional imaginative roles. The greatest performance may mean crossing over into madness (acid as a door leading to sanity or madness).

Inauthenticity / Authenticity characterized *not* by continuity but by ABRUPTNESS.

** Idea of Rolling Stones – co-presence of radical uprootedness with radical individualization. (utter fragmentation of reality!)

* The pivotal character of the Rolling Stones – the revolution in sensibility associated with rock music. Reality the collective fantasy of a technological worldview (*nihilism*).

* FLUIDIFICATION is REIFICATION (a radical assault on conventional values the key to transformation of life).

Dominance of possibilities over norms (paralysis of possibilities for the former, and a reality for the latter).

Routine as a tranquilizing nightmare.

* Search for an authentic *'average everydayness'* is this generation's counter-possibility to meaninglessness and nihilism.

** Public opinion dissolves the selfhood of each of its members (behind each one's back as it were) – conscious / unconscious giving up of self.

*** The revolution in personal, sexual, social values is deeply disturbing – to be taken through a *transcendent conversion experience* is to be BLASTED free of everything we have been, everything we have known. Preparation of a *Da* for *Sein*.

Authentic 'average everydayness' = the DISSOLUTION of what we would consider everydayness for a community of people. There are an infinite number of average everydaynesses just as beginning with Riemann we saw in mathematics that there are an infinite number of GEOMETRIES (depending upon whether the sum of the internal angles of a triangle is greater than or less than 180°). Thus there are potentially as many 'average everydaynesses' as there are existing people on the earth at a given time (this is similar to the notion that there are potentially as many RELIGIONS as there are existing individuals).

* The *public is enemy no. one* (1) – *Rolling Stones essential message*.

* To really listen to the Rolling Stones means one must hear their music with much more than just one's ears.

What is the meaning of this vast existential consequence for all collective institutions (such as political life, social life whether communist or capitalist, etc.? It means COLLAPSE, the emergence of some kind of viable anarchy).

{
* Inauthentic everydayness = a LEVELLING
* *Authentic* everydayness = an OVERLAP
}

("Happening" is an overlap)

** **Addenda** –

* The Rolling Stones will HAPPEN in the book that comes THROUGH me. The TEXT is the thing that has happened.

* Bertrand Russell – "I would rather be mad with the truth than sane with lies."

* Heidegger disposes of existentialism in one sentence – "only EXISTING can solve and work out the question of existence in its *ontic, existentiell* sense."

* Music is the POETRY of this generation.

* Because *Dasein* cannot ground itself, it must *always* be a Rolling Stone… (LTS).

"As in the worldview of the Hopi Indians, consciousness, energy, and MATTER form a continuum" (…subjective / objective distinctions about reality are incorrect).
>	William Irwin Thompson, "Planetary Vistas," *Harpers Magazine*, Dec. 1977 (p. 75)

* "Yet as soon as man GIVES THOUGHT to his homelessness, it is a misery no longer."
>	M. Heidegger, *Poetry, Language, Thought* (p. 161)

"How many criers are inquirers?" (LTS)

"Growing means this: to open oneself up to the breadth of heaven and to sink one's roots into the darkness of earth…"
>	M. Heidegger, *The Pathway* (p. 3)

(The secret of long, slow growth)

Rolling Stones' Trademark – an Excursus

Rolling Stones' Trademark = tongue of KALI (see K. Richard's Rolling Stone interview, August 19, 1971). In the original Sanskrit Kali means TIME, RIVER, but it also is associated with DEATH. The Tongue of Kali in effect is a Rolling Stones' YANTRA (a *visual* MANTRA or sacred syllable like "AUM"). Kali is the matron goddess of both Hindu and Buddhist TANTRISM. She simultaneously exudes awesome beauty and terror (usually she is depicted as dancing on top of a vast ashen graveyard of littered human bones, a necklace of skulls adorning her dark body, her six arms in various iconographic gestures of eerie aggressiveness).

Unlike Yoga, Tantrism is the radical attempt to achieve enlightenment (whether Śunyata or Brahman) VIA the SENSES – particularly through ritualized SEXUAL EXCESS (the famous Tibetan YAB-YUM tantric coupling of male-female symbolizes in anthropomorphic form the interdependence and interpenetration of all of reality). It must be noted further that Madhyamika (meaning "middle way") Buddhism is the formal philosophical underpinning of Buddhist tantrism. The Madhyamika School has been wrongly called *Ucchedavada* or NIHILISTIC because it insists on the RADICAL IMPERMANENCE of all reality to the exclusion of any and all absolutes whatsoever – indeed it is even willing to negate its own formulations in its process of total DE-ABSOLUTIZATION. The ultimate non-differentiation of Nirvana and Samsara means in effect that there is no ultimate reality, and that wisdom and ignorance are only pseudo-distinctions.

Also, according to the systematic formulations of Indian mythology, our own age is the KALI YUGA, the Age of COLLAPSE and DISINTEGRATION during which DHARMA (meaning "rightness," "order," "duty") precariously stands on only one of its four legs (Dharma is here depicted as a sacred cow standing squarely on four legs at the beginning of the four-part cosmic time-cycle). Thus the Kali Yuga is a shorthand symbol for the imminent collapse of all order (both "divine" and human). Hence the Rolling Stones' tongue is not merely a conventional symbol expressing lewdness, defiance, and rejection, but more importantly it is a philosophical symbol symbolizing TIME, DEATH, IMPERMANENCE, and consequently FINITUDE.

How is the TERROR of TIME related to the RADICAL UPROOTEDNESS of the epoch? This is the as yet unasked question that arises in thinking about the relation of the tongue of Kali to the Rolling Stones themselves (one is here reminded of a remark that Heidegger has made regarding Nietzsche that seems equally applicable to the SHRILL extremism of both Tantrism and the Rolling Stones: He had to endure the agony of having to scream).

*Authors who may be consulted further on Tantrism: Zimmer, Eliade, Guenther, Bharati (née Fischer)

The Question of Joujouka

Attar – Arabic meaning "perfume maker," also the name of a 13th century Muslim poet. *Attar* is definitely a Sufi symbol referring to the *divine essence*.

Books on Sufism to check –

1. *Hindu and Muslim Mysticism* by Richard Zaehner.
2. *The Way of the Sufi* et. al. by Idries Shah.

Additional books to check:

1. *The Process* by Brion Gysin.
2. *The Ticket That Exploded* by W. Burroughs.
3. Anything by Paul Bowles.

The music of Joujouka (being originally the court music of North Africa and even of Muslim Spain) = Cthonian elements (pre-Muslim, the matriarchical EARTH religion found in Aisha Hamouka, Dionysian mystery in the goat god Bou Jeloud) and Sufi elements. This music is TRANSCENDENTAL insofar as its purport is the ALTERATION of consciousness, the inducement of TRANCE through polyrythmic subtle variations.

* Brian Jones looked to this music as a vehicle for transcending the impossible contradictions and stagnation currently gripping the "soul" of Western civilization? This point needs to be explored.

The whole phenomenon of Dionysian mystery religions (the Orphic cults, etc.) need to be looked into (everything from Dodd's *The Greeks and the Irrational* to Nietzsche's *The Birth of Tragedy*).

Apollo – EGO vs. Dionysus – SHATTERING of the EGO

Nietzsche's Uebermensch a linking of Apollo and Dionysus (Nietzsche in fact calls his god Dionysus)

Annex: Part C – Full Circle

The Soundtrack of Modern Times…120

Blaze of Glory…122

The Beatles-Stones…125

THE SOUNDTRACK OF MODERN TIMES – A TRIANGLE

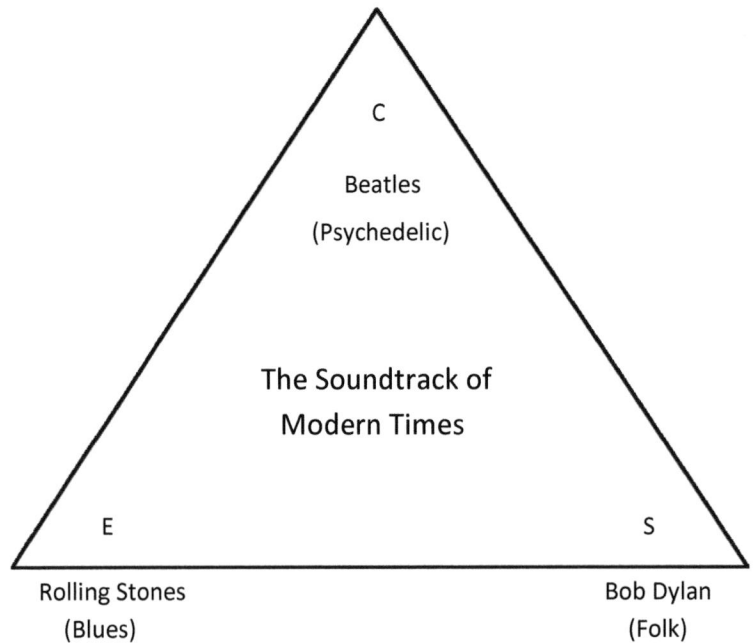

Key Albums

1. <u>Rolling Stones</u> –
Aftermath
Satanic Majesties Request (original working title: *Cosmic Christmas*)
Beggars Banquet

2. <u>Bob Dylan</u> –
Bringing It All Back Home
Highway 61 Revisited
Blonde on Blonde

3. <u>Beatles</u> –
Rubber Soul
Revolver
Sgt. Pepper

THE SOUNDTRACK OF MODERN TIMES – NOTES

The Mount Olympus of Rock Culture.
(Rolling Stones, Bob Dylan, Beatles)

A Triple Foundation of Musical Forces.
(Blues Tradition, Folk Tradition, Psychedelic Tradition – India: *Sitar*)

1) E = the EXISTENTIAL (the REBEL) – the PERSONAL.
2) S = the SOCIAL (the PROPHET) – the PROTEST.
3) C = the COSMIC (the SAGE) – the UNIVERSAL.

"We talked about… how music was used by the common people to answer and embrace every aspect of the *human condition*." (Sam Cutler)

"As Mick Jagger observed at the time, 'The *Stones* might speak to one's personal condition in a way that the Beatles did not, but the Beatles were UNIVERSAL.'" (Oliver Julien)

"The sixties seem like a golden age to us because, relative to now, they were. At their heart, the counter cultural revolution against acquisitive selfishness – and, in particular, the hippies' unfashionable perception that we can change the world only by changing ourselves – looks in retrospect like a LAST GASP of the Western SOUL." (to be more authentic) (Ian Macdonald)

**The Tragedy of Post-Rock Culture – the AMPUTATION of the COSMIC…

Blaze of Glory

Acid (LSD) is Truth
And pray thee what is Truth?
Unity of man
Unity of Life (*élan vital*)
Unity of the Planet
Unity of the COSMOS
A Rock & Roll PANTHEISM
(a working hypothesis)

From Sgt. Pepper
"I get by with a little help from my friends,
 I get high with a little help from my friends,
 Going to try with a little help from my friends.
 What do you see when you turn out the light,
 I can't tell you, but I know it's mine."
"Newspaper taxis appear on the shore,
 Waiting to take you away.
 Climb in the back with your head in the clouds,
 And you're gone.
 Lucy in the sky with diamonds."
"Try to realize it's all within yourself no-one else
 Can make you change
 And to see you're really only very small,
 And life flows on within you and without you.
 When you've seen beyond yourself – then
 You may find, peace of mind, is waiting there –
 And the time will come when you see
 We're all ONE, and life flows on within you and without you."

*From *Satanic Majesties**

"Why don't we sing this song all together
  Open our heads, let the pictures come
  And if we close all our eyes together
  Then we will see where we all come from"
"Oh daddy be proud of your planet,
  Oh mummy be proud of your sun" (repeat)
"Pictures of us spin the circling sun
  Pictures of us showing that we're all ONE"

*The temporary DISRUPTION of ordinary, average, everyday consciousness by COSMIC, *psychedelic* consciousness.

*This is what *Sgt. Pepper* & *Satanic Majesties* have in COMMON. = The *Beatles Stones*.

THE POWER OF FLOWER

"Or play the game existence to the end.
Of the beginning, of the beginning.
Of the beginning, of the beginning."
Revolver
OR
A DEISTIC rock & roll PANTHEISM.
DOMINUS ILLUMINATIO MEA
The Lord is my LIGHT.
(Psalm XXVII)
*A Theism of Ceremonial Reverence (*élan vital*)*

Recommended Reading

* Philosophy

Martin Heidegger, *Being and Time*, Translated by John Macquarrie and Edward Robinson. Harper Collins, 2008.

Martin Heidegger, *Being and Time*, Translated by Joan Stambaugh. SUNY Press, 2010.

Magda King, *A Guide to Heidegger's Being and Time*. SUNY Press, 2001.

Richard E. Palmer, *Hermeneutics*. Northwestern University Press, 1975.

James M. Demske, *Being, Man & Death – A Key to Heidegger*. The University Press of Kentucky, 1970.

* Music

Paul Trynka, *Brian Jones*. Viking, 2014.

Bill Wyman, *Stone Alone*. Viking Penguin, 1990.

Bill Wyman, *Blues Odyssey*. DK, 2001 (with 2 CD's).

Bill Wyman, *Rolling With the Stones*. DK, 2002.

Greil Marcus, *Like a Rolling Stone*. Faber & Faber, 2005.

* <u>Optional – Additional Interest</u>

Richard Havers, *The Stones in the Park*. Haynes Publishing, 2009.

Jim DeRogatis & Greg Kot, *The Beatles vs. The Rolling Stones*. Voyageur Press, 2010.

Jann S. Wenner, *Lennon Remembers* (New Edition). Verso, 2000.

Bob Dylan, *Chronicles: Volume One*. Pocket Books, 2004.

Wallace Fowlie, *Rimbaud and Jim Morrison*. Duke University Press, 1993.

"I COLLECT MY TOOLS:
Sight, smell, touch, taste,
hearing, intellect. Night
has fallen, the day's work is done…" –
Nikos Kazantzakis, *Report to Greco* (p. 12)

The Spirit of '76 – A Biographical Sketch

Laurence Tucker Stallings III was born in Hollywood, California on March 6, 1939 to a movie family, spent his formative years in the Southern California area, and has had a rich and varied life. He fulfilled his military obligation by serving in the U.S. Marine Corps, and then went on to Stanford University as an undergraduate where he was awarded a B.A. degree in Political Science – International Relations. Inspired by the shocking death of President John F. Kennedy, he went back into government service again, and joined the U.S. Peace Corps. His duty completed, once more he went back into academics as a graduate student at the East-West Center, University of Hawaii, where he studied Comparative Philosophy, and was awarded an equivalent M.A. degree in Comparative East-West Philosophy, with a specialization in Contemporary European and Indian Philosophy. He then moved to Long Island, New York, and worked full time as a journalist (cultural editor and news correspondent) for the *Moniebogue Press*, a regional newspaper in Westhampton Beach for almost a year, in order to save money for a permanent move to Germany. And there he has remained (Tübingen – 1974) ever since, starting a second life, and putting down new roots. Still active at the German-American Institute after all these years (25), he is now basking in the bliss, or afterglow, of a semi-retired life…

An American Dream?

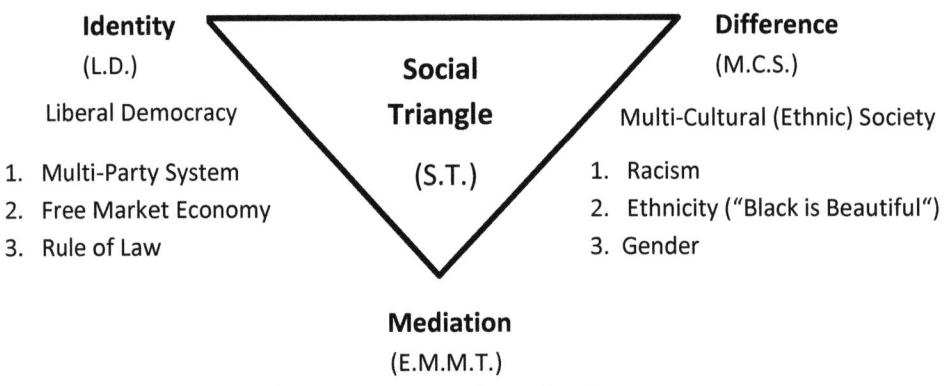

Identity   **Social**   **Difference**
(L.D.)   **Triangle**   (M.C.S.)

Liberal Democracy   (S.T.)   Multi-Cultural (Ethnic) Society

1. Multi-Party System   1. Racism
2. Free Market Economy   2. Ethnicity ("Black is Beautiful")
3. Rule of Law   3. Gender

Mediation
(E.M.M.T.)
Electronic Mass Media Technology
("The Global Village,"
"The Medium is the Message")

Foundations
1. Film – Hollywood
2. Music – Rock & Roll
3. Sport – Football (Soccer)
(A MINIMAL WORLD CULTURE)

An American Institution –
<u>Beach Boys</u> – *Endless Summer,*
Pet Sounds, Smile
<u>Grateful Dead</u> – *Live/Dead,*
Workingman's Dead,
American Beauty

d.a.i.
Deutsch-Amerikanisches Institut
(German-American Institute),
Tübingen, 2002

Personal/General

Laurence Stallings

On the occasion of its fiftieth anniversary, in the shadow of the one-year aftermath to the horrible events of September 11th, I have been asked to write some timely remarks about the d.a.i. and my relation to this noble institute.

Although having been engaged in a broad range of activities in my fourteen years here, from teaching to taking out the trash, it is always as an ambassador of good will, a representative of my country and its culture that I have regarded myself and tried to project onto others.

In its multiple function as a language and cultural institute connected by a library, the d.a.i. has been not just a place of work, but a second home, a "home away from home" for me. And as we all know, home is where the heart is.

In its triple capacity as a teaching tool, a cultural connection, and a mental mother ship, working in and using the library has been in particular an invaluable treasure house of riches, both personally and pedagogically.
Indeed the library has proved to be for me and my classes the master-key that unlocks the double-door of language and culture, of words and worldview, and values as the glue holding and cementing everything together – the give and take of perception and expression, and the rock bottom, the bedrock of who and what we are.

"To imagine a language (game) is to imagine a form of life, a culture" – these few words by Ludwig Wittgenstein have gone a long way for me in teaching English (Upper Intermediate and Advanced levels), beginning to teach a better understanding of some fundamental aspects of American history, society, and culture – such as the American Dream and the American Way of Life. An obvious final lesson – anyone thinking they know everything about American culture can only be misinformed.

Using a very simple but creative dynamic between general knowledge and current events has been very fruitful over the years in coming to grips with some very basic facts and challenges of American life – such as the ongoing

tension between liberal democracy (identity), and an increasingly multi-ethnic, multi-cultural socio order (difference), and a continuing revolution in perception by electronic, mass-media technology, which is fueling the emergence of a new popular global culture (mediation) based upon a three-fold foundation of film, music, and sport.

And now, by a not so subtle shift of gears, let me turn to the personal and try to put some flesh and blood onto the skeleton of my previous remarks. Countless memories, events, situations, persons, encounters crowd into my mind, demanding, begging impatiently, jostling for expression, however partial and imperfect – how could I possibly do an iota of justice to even the least of them? It has been a long, rich, overflowing fourteen years: the matter-of-fact Doors' presentation that turned into a wild, stomping, wine drinking dance party; the tears of admiration and wonder of students at the close of the sixty-minute Albert Einstein documentary, "How I See The World"; the blinding flash of insight so obvious in everyones' eyes after a reading and discussion of Bertrand Russell's simple but moving one-page foreword to his "Autobiography, What I Have Lived For?"; my "o.k., but wrong" humorous reply to a student's "Yesterday, I have eaten in the mensa" formulation in a grammar exercise, stressing the difference between Past and Present Perfect verb tense usage – these are but some of the things swimming before my dazzled eyes in all their random nebulosity...

Let me just conclude, all too abruptly, that it has been an honor as well as a privilege for me to have had the good fortune of working at this institute for all these years, and hopefully even more of a pleasure in the years to come.